THE WINTER WAR

THE WINTER WAR

THE RUSSO-FINNISH CONFLICT, 1939-40

ELOISE ENGLE AND LAURI PAANANEN

CHARLES SCRIBNER'S SONS
NEW YORK

947.1

Printed in the United States of America
Library of Congress Catalog Card Number 72–1217
SBN 684–13047–5

To our mothers in their northern cheering sections: Elina Paananen in Stockholm, Sweden,
and Lois Thomas in Anchorage, Alaska.

CONTENTS

PREFACE

Were you to travel from the Arctic Ocean to the city of Leningrad, along the Russo-Finnish border in the year 1939, you would have had a complex journey. The frontier itself separating the two countries was little more than a wide swath cut through the forests, or a line snaking around lakes and rivers. Dotted along the way were groups of border guards at various crossroads or other areas that seemed important for surveillance. On the Russian side, there had been large troop concentrations of late; railroads and highways had snuggled cozily against Finland's eastern border.

These border guards did not like each other, operating as they did under full view of one another's activities. They were described by a foreign correspondent as being "like angry bulls on neighboring farms, separated only by a barbed-wire fence." This in itself was not an uncommon factor; political geography has often produced border squabbles, particularly when opposing political views are involved. But this border was too close to Leningrad for Soviet security. Or so the Russians claimed.

It was here in the late autumn of 1939 that the so-called Winter War began. The Russians did not plan on Finnish resistance to a take-over of their country. Nikita Khrushchev said, in his memoirs, "All we had to do was raise our voice a little bit and the Finns would obey. If that didn't work, we could fire one shot and the Finns would put up their hands and surrender. Or so we thought."[1]

The former Soviet premier continues: "The Finns turned out to be good warriors. We soon realized we had bitten off more than we could chew."[2] For 105 days in 1939–40 one of the toughest campaigns of the early World War II era was fought.

[1]Nikita Khrushchev, *Khrushchev Remembers* (Boston: Little, Brown and Company, 1970), p. 152.
[2]Ibid., p. 153.

In the context of global war, it was relatively small and yet an estimated 2 million Russian and Finnish soldiers took part. It cost the Soviets a possible 1,000 airplanes and 2,300 tanks. It was not until 1970 that Khrushchev's memoirs revealed the loss of a million Russian lives in the Winter War.

With the Finnish resistance to the Big Bear's aggression came world-wide moral protest, universal sympathy, expulsion of the USSR from the League of Nations, and a Nazi secret chuckle over the fiasco in the north. Khrushchev says, "The Germans were watching with undisguised glee as we took a drubbing from the Finns."[3] Here at last was the display of the Red Army in action. It was a campaign that perhaps changed the pattern of World War II, if not the history of the world.

Today, the Western world remembers the time "when the Finns beat the Russians" but the highlights have dimmed with the passing years. Western war colleges still request information on Winter War tactics, and in Sweden a textbook on the subject is the standard reference—not that any country would try to duplicate the feats of that era. The Finns today, because of their precarious geographical position, prefer to shrug their shoulders with characteristic stoicism and say, "Well, we lived through it. Now, let us go forward and not think about the past." Only the old war-horses in Finland sometimes reminisce about it over a late-night schnapps.

For the sake of simplicity in referring to Russian officers of general rank, the authors have chosen to use the Finnish designations. During the Winter War the Red Army experimented with such ranks as ComBrig (Commander Brigade), ComDiv (Commander Division), and ArmCom (Army Commander). These terms were dropped after the Winter War and generals became generals again.

This is not an authorized history and it has not been directed, subsidized, commissioned, or in any way controlled by any agency, government or private. But we must add that we have received great assistance from many individuals without whose help this book could not have been written. We owe every one of them a great debt of gratitude. At the same time, we take full responsibility for any errors of fact or interpretation.

ELOISE ENGLE
LAURI PAANANEN

[3]Ibid.

 # ACKNOWLEDGMENTS

When research on the Winter War first began, the authors fully realized that without co-operation and help from many sources, Finland's epic struggle could not be accurately and properly related thirty years after it all happened. It was only through the enthusiasm and dedication of those special people who gave freely of their time that this book was possible.

Our deep gratitude goes to Elina Paananen, the co-author's mother, who searched the book stores in both Stockholm and Helsinki for new and old volumes of Winter War material. She supplied clippings, photos, and always the badly needed moral support along the way. Her help was invaluable.

For Russian and German translations, the authors were fortunate in finding Lydia Marshalka, Latvian, who is a translator for the Library of Congress. Her father was chief of police in Moscow until the Bolshevik revolution. Lydia was an opera singer in Latvia until the Russians took over her country, when she fled to England, then to the United States. She is now an American citizen. For these reasons, she did much work "above and beyond the call of duty."

Colonel Martti Frick, Embassy of Finland, Washington, D.C., was extremely generous with his time in sharing his personal experiences of the Winter War. He also provided the valuable tactics book, written by Colonel Y. A. Järvinen, which even today is used as a handbook in the Swedish military academies. Further appreciation is given to Colonel Järvinen's son, Major Olli Yki-Järvinen, Ministry of Foreign Affairs in

Helsinki, for permission to use his late father's reflections in this book's epilogue.

Colonel Keijo Mikola, Finnish army (ret.), formerly with the War Historical Institute in Helsinki, was personally acquainted with many of the officers of the Winter War era. He supplied the authors with biographical information along with other valuable data for use as cross reference. Commander Aarno Koivisto, Finnish navy, furnished the authors material on the navy's role during the conflict. Major Pertti Jokinen, Assistant Military Attaché, Finnish Embassy, loaned a very helpful book and provided liaison contacts. Colonel Olavi Lehti, Military Attaché at the Finnish Embassy supplied helpful first-hand information.

Photographs and maps to illustrate a thirty-year-old war were difficult to come by. Fortunately, Werner Söderström, publishers in Helsinki, most generously provided a number of fine photos that have not been seen outside of Finnish publications. Mrs. Sinikka Kurikka handled the authors' requests with efficiency and friendliness. Also, the Finnish Tourist Bureau, the Institute of Military History, and the Headquarters, Training Division, in Helsinki supplied the authors with further photos and biographical material.

Much of the research was centered at the Library of Congress where Mr. Legare H. B. Obear, Chief of the Loan Division, allowed the authors to borrow books in several languages for this project. Pauli Pajupuro, along with Esko Lehmus of Lehmus Oy in Tampere, Finland, made available the Finnish war cartoons. Jaakko Jahnukainen, well-known producer of Finnish television documentaries, was instrumental in arranging very helpful contacts with knowledgeable historians. . . .

The Fairfax County (Virginia) libraries, and in particular the Woodrow Wilson branch in Falls Church, Virginia, always stood ready to find needed material, regardless of the sometimes strange nature of the requests. There was also assistance in military terminology from Army information officers at the Pentagon.

Words cannot express the authors' gratitude for the advice, consultation, and encouragement of the fine husband-and-wife writer team, who write under the pen names Erick Berry and Herbert Best.

 # INTRODUCTION

In 1924, when the Finnish National Airlines (FINNAIR) first began operations, pilots flying Junker F-13 monoplanes over the white-blanketed countryside of their homeland often became confused about where to land. Wearing fur-lined helmets, goggles, and with white scarves fluttering in the wind, they would swoop low over a farm field and shout, "Where is Finland?"

By 1939 a great many more people were asking that same question. Suddenly Finland was a very important pawn in world politics.

Not only, "Where is Finland?" but, "What is Finland all about?"

Finland is that rarity in the world, an underpopulated country with some 4.5 million people scattered over 130,000 square miles. A land of lake and forest, it is eight times the size of Denmark. In wintertime the country is very cold, with one third of the land above the Arctic Circle. It is bordered on the east by Soviet Russia and on the west by Sweden. The only thing that keeps it from being a Frozen North or another Antarctic is the warming influence of the Gulf Stream swinging south into the Baltic and north into the Arctic Ocean. Some northern ports, such as Petsamo, are never icebound. It is a country where only the toughest of people could survive. Only an extremely powerful and confident aggressor would dare attack it in wintertime.

The Finns are a pioneer people. They first entered their country during the earlier Iron Age, traveling across the narrow gulf from Estonia and Latvia. They are not Nordics, nor are they Mongols as many still suppose them to be. Their national language bears resemblance to the ancient

Finno-Ugric tongue, including Estonian and Hungarian, and their national epic, the *Kalevala*, which so appealed to Longfellow, is based on folk poetry and mythology of the Finno-Ugrians.

When headlines around the world first began reporting the Soviet-Finnish boundary disputes, people only hazily understood the country of Finland and the people who lived there. Finns often traveled abroad but few Western tourists made the effort to visit this out-of-the-way little republic. Americans thought fondly of the painfully honest people as being the only debtors of World War I who had insisted on paying their bill to the United States.

Music lovers throughout the world had been thrilled by the music of Jean Sibelius, whose *Finlandia* so movingly portrayed his homeland, the political tensions and wars, and the spirit of the people. Finnish athletes in the 1936 Olympic games in Berlin won seven gold, six silver, and six bronze medals, placing fourth in the entire world, following Germany, the United States, and Italy. Earlier, in the 1920s, long-distance runner Paavo Nurmi had become a legend in three Olympics for his speed and endurance. In the 1930s beauty queens from Finland, with their lithe figures and blond, blue-eyed loveliness, captured more than their share of prizes, and many people had begun to suspect that Finns were not always fighting bears with knives or otherwise conducting themselves as barbarians.

It was known that the Finns had a passion for cleanliness, but their sauna baths were often viewed by conservative Americans with considerable suspicion; it seemed that entire families shared the ritual—without clothes! And oddly enough, wherever a Finn traveled, lived, or formed an acquaintance, his distinct personality made an impression.

For centuries Finland had been a punching bag for her powerful neighbors; first Sweden, then Russia. Because she was without any cohesive political or social structure to connect her widely scattered settlements, Finland was gradually annexed by the Swedes during the medieval era. By the end of the fourteenth century Finland was, in effect, a province of the Swedish Kingdom. Swedish political and cultural institutions were imposed on the newly acquired subjects; even the Swedish language was used for all official, educational, and literary purposes. It was only through sheer stubborness that the Finnish masses refused to give up their ancient language, so that at the peak of Swedish power, not more than 20 percent of the Finns spoke Swedish either as a mother tongue or as an adopted one. Later Finland became a dual-language country.

During the three centuries before Finland was ceded to Russia she was involved in war for a total of more than eighty years, and at times further weakened by famine or plague. Twelve major wars were fought between Sweden and Russia on Finnish soil, and during the Thirty Years' War Finland was forced to provide one-third of Gustavus Adolphus's army. Between 1710 and 1721 Finland was partly or completely occupied by Russian armies whose vandalism and destruction brought normal life to a standstill, ruined whole towns, and reduced the Finnish population by a quarter.

The cession of Finland to Russia in 1809 was part of the redrawing of the map of Europe which took place during the Napoleonic Wars. During the 1800s Finland as a self-governing Grand Duchy provided Russia with some four hundred generals and admirals and a steady stream of other officers. The most notable was Field Marshal Carl Gustav Mannerheim who entered the Imperial Guards in 1890. He later led the Finns to independence in 1918 and fought the Russians during the Winter War.

Although social life between the two peoples was cordial, a number of Finns became concerned that such harmony would lead to total Russification. The slogan of the time—"We are no longer Swedes, we will not become Russians, so let us be Finns"—was echoed through the years but the political movement never matured to any great extent.

With Alexander II's assassination in 1881 came a whole new era of oppression under Alexander III. The Russians took over control of Finnish universities, the law courts, and the press, but the worst was yet to come under the reign of Nicholas II. The new czar's Governor-General, Nicholas Bobrikov, appointed Russians to all administrative positions in Finland and Russian became the official language of the country. All Finnish legislation was transferred to the Russian government, the Finnish army was absorbed by the imperial forces, and any Finn who resisted these orders was sent to Siberia. A favorite sport of the Russians during Bobrikov's period of power was bull-whipping civilians from horseback in the Helsinki squares. By 1914 the degree of self-government the Finns had known came to an end. Hatred for Russia was deep and seething.

During this period, small activist groups had been working to overthrow the Russian rule and establish Finnish independence. Because she had no army during World War I, Finland used this time to develop her own military strength. With Sweden proclaiming her neutrality, the Finns turned to Germany, who was then at war with Russia.

The Germans gladly responded to the plea for help and in 1915–16 secretly accepted 2,000 young Finns at their Feldmeister School in Lockstedt, near Hamburg, where they were formed into the 27th Royal Prussian Jaeger Battalion. The first basic unit of 183 Finns was led by a handsome German major, Maximilian Bayer, whose severe training whipped the young individualists into a first-class group of military leaders.

The impact of the March, 1917, revolution in Russia left Finland wondering what her position would be. On December 6 Finland formally declared her independence and on the last day of 1917 Lenin's government recognized the new state. Finland now stood alone before the storms that were raging abroad and brewing at home. .

Technically, the transfer of power from Russia to Finland was a simple exercise, because Finland had long been a separate unit from both Sweden and Russia. She had her own democratic constitution and governmental machinery, but politically, she lacked experience. The years without normal government had created serious social problems and many reforms were long overdue.

In January, 1918, a wave of terror ushered in a tragic civil war. To oppose the terrorists was the White Guard led by (then) General Mannerheim, who had recently returned from Russia.

Although the issues were mainly domestic, there were still some 20,000 Russian soldiers in Finland that had not been withdrawn and who had joined forces with the Finnish Red Guard. It became Mannerheim's primary aim to rid Finland of these Bolshevik troops, but the Finnish government, in its impatience, requested aid from Germany. Against Mannerheim's wishes 8,000 German troops landed in Finland in April and by the middle of May, the Independence War was all over.

Finland had avoided communism but had emerged as a distinctly pro-German state. There were many unsolved constitutional problems and political divisions which would take years to heal. The armistice in November brought World War I to a fortunate end and Finland was faced squarely with the independence which she had so long desired yet which she had begun to fear when it was within her grasp.

Eventually a republican form of government was agreed upon and in July the first president of Finland, Professor K. J. Ståhlberg, took office.

The Treaty of Tartu officially ended the Russian domination; independent Finland was born, not with a silver spoon but with a dagger in her mouth.

On the Russian side, the Communists bitterly hated the Finns' stubborn, unyielding struggle for the right to live their own lives. They constantly regretted "giving" Finland her independence but many were convinced that clever subversion, propaganda, and economic pressure would bring the Finns to heel.

As for the Finns, they had developed an almost fanatical loathing of communism, and a sense of frustrated superiority towards Russians. Their knowledge of the Russian way of thinking and acting came from long association rather than from any similarity in ways of living, outlook, or common origin.

In addition to personality conflicts, the Finns felt they had established a much higher culture and living standard than had the Russians during the past twenty years; they had eased their poverty load and compensated for their production and trade inequities by forming one of the most successful co-operative systems in the world. They did not want to be pulled down to the Russian level just as things were beginning to seem brighter.

Because of their land and history, Finns were extremely complicated personalities. Wayward, stubborn, often enigmatic individualists, they had emerged from their uncertain parentage with their own language, dialects, and racial eccentricities. Their diversity of appearance and temperament was greater than in many countries with ten times their population, so that the "blond, blue-eyed Finn" of the travel folder could not be considered representative of national type.

In spite of the several kinds of Finns who had reached their country by different routes, settled in one area, and remained there, all shared the national characteristic of *sisu* which loosely translated means guts and the equally strong trait of tenacity. Both are admirable in the form of determination to overcome all difficulties; but exasperating in the form of downright cussedness. These qualities had helped the Finns surmount historic and geographic obstacles. Should an enemy attack occur, these traits would be the people's chief support.

PROLOGUE

In November, 1939, the sky over the Kremlin was cold, gray, and gloomy. The people in Moscow, Leningrad, and in other parts of the Soviet Union were somewhat confused but nevertheless excited about the latest "liberation" plan. With the might of the powerful Red Army, the people of Finland would soon be set free. Soviet leaders were confident that the task would be easy.

The conference room was brightly lit as General Kirill A. Meretskov, commander of the Russian forces committed to the Finnish campaign, stood and smiled confidently to greet G. I. Kulik and L. Z. Mekhlis, deputy people's commissars of defense. The only solemn face was that of Chief Marshal of Artillery N. N. Voronov.

The meeting proceeded as Kulik addressed Voronov. "You have come at the right time. Do you know about the dangerous situation in Finland?"

Voronov nodded.

"Have you given any thought to the number of shells that will be needed for possible combat operations on the Karelian Isthmus and to the north of Lake Ladoga? What kind of artillery support is needed? What can we count on?"

Voronov glanced at his enthusiastic comrades, then carefully replied: "In my opinion, everything depends on the situation. Are you planning to defend or attack? With what forces and in what sectors? By the way, how much time is being allotted for the operation?"

The pause was only momentary, "Between ten and twelve days."

1

Voronov said, "I will be happy if everything can be resolved within two or three months."

Everyone laughed.

"Marshal Voronov," Kulik said sternly. "You are ordered to base all of your estimates on the assumption that the operation will last twelve days."[1]

[1]N. N. Voronov, *Na sluzhbe voennoi* (Moscow, 1963), pp. 136-37.

1 | "IT IS NOT POSSIBLE FOR YOU [IN FINLAND] TO REMAIN NEUTRAL"

Cold wind swept across the wooded, snow-covered fields of the Karelian Isthmus. It stung the men's exposed faces with little needles of icy spray that blew from the ground and from the trees. But the Russian soldiers, singing around their campfires, playing accordians and balalaikas and warming their chilled bodies with liberal rations of vodka, were light-hearted and gay. In a few days they would liberate Finland from the evils of capitalism; they would be heroes as soon as they crossed the border and made their purposes known.

General Meretskov, forty-two-year-old commander of the Russian 7th, 8th, 9th, and 14th Armies, was pleased with his inspection tour of that afternoon. As he emerged from his staff car, however, he was thankful for his fur-lined cape which smartly covered his olive brown tunic of light-weight material. The troops, with their summer uniforms, seemed quite comfortable at the moment. Overcoats would not be needed, since the campaign was scheduled to last only a few days.

Hundreds of tanks lined the network of roads that led into Finnish Karelia. Because of the cold snap, engines were periodically run so they would be kept warm. The tanks were ready to lead the massive infantry forces when Meretskov gave the order to move. Unfortunately the short hours of daylight at this time of year would prevent extensive air operations in support of his initial attacks, but there was sufficient time for Soviet planes to paralyze the cities on bombing runs from Estonian bases. Soviet bombers and fighters numbered 3,000, to neutralize the Finnish air force of 162 antiquated biplanes and Fokkers. Also, the air arm had

3

done a splendid job of reconnaissance these past few weeks. Roads, ports, industrial areas and fortifications had been duly photographed in spite of Finnish protests against overflying. Intelligence reports had indicated that the Finns had only a few old light-weight tanks and probably fewer than 100 small-caliber anti-panzer guns.

It was the night of November 25, 1939, and although war had not formally been declared and in fact never would be by the Russians, it was only a matter of waiting for final word that plans had proceeded as scheduled.[1] The awaited "incident" should take place the next day, and four days later the mighty Red armies under Meretskov's command would swarm into Finland. At the Karelian Isthmus alone more than 250,000 soldiers were overflowing the local barracks. There were Red troops as far as the eye could see along the 90-mile front. This was almost as many combatants as the entire country of Finland could muster, even if old men and boys were included. In spite of the fact that troops marching toward the border in the north were experiencing casualties from frostbite and cold, the general anticipated no real difficulties with the Finnish campaign. A quick victory would insure the plaudits of Stalin, Molotov, and Communist Party members all over the world.

General Meretskov had come a long way from his peasant origin. A factory worker in Moscow, he had entered the Party in May, 1917, as a member of the Red Guard. The following year he had become a political commissar in the Red Army. Steadily he had worked his way through the hierarchy of the system and by 1938 had become commander of the Leningrad Military District.

On this important evening he studied the wall map that hung in his headquarters. The only serious fortification that he would have to combat along the entire 800-mile Russo-Finnish border lay in the 90-mile front on the Karelian Isthmus between the Gulf of Finland and Lake Ladoga. The strength and fortifications of this Mannerheim Line were somewhat uncertain in Meretskov's mind but the challenge of breaching it was an intriguing one. The press likened it to the Maginot Line in France and would certainly call attention to his victories there. The 600-mile front north of Lake Ladoga to the Arctic Ocean would be virtually defenseless against the twenty powerful divisions he placed in those key areas.

The Karelian Isthmus would be strongly defended, but with the fall of

[1]The Soviets would recognize only the puppet government of Finnish Marxist Otto Kuusinen, set up after the invasion began.

Viipuri, Finland's second largest city, the Russian timetable of conquest would be nearly complete. There would be easy access to Helsinki, the capital, and from then on it would be all over. Orders were that a screeching halt must be made once the Swedish border was reached. There was to be no violation of that country's steadfast neutrality.

Yes, the isthmus would have to be taken as quickly as possible. There were many points in Meretskov's favor. The weather, for instance, had frozen the ground hard, but as yet there was very little snow. The lakes and rivers were beginning to freeze and soon the ice would be strong enough to support the Soviet heavy equipment. The network of roads on the isthmus was gaining in firmness and it would be a simple matter to construct new roads as long as the snow cover remained thin. The Karelian Isthmus itself was considered the Finn's Thermopylae because its narrowest part was only 45 miles wide. Lakes and marshes divided the terrain into what amounted to passes but the lack of rock foundation made it unsuitable for permanent fortifications. It would be good going for tanks because there were few hills of any size; frozen potato and wheat fields would make excellent battle areas for heavy artillery and armored vehicles.

General Meretskov had no way of knowing that the weather he was enjoying that evening would soon change, and that the Finnish winter of 1939 would be the second coldest since the year 1828. His Red armies were about to plunge into a frozen hell.

Across the border the people of Finland had just about dug in for the winter. November had turned the skies to gray. For weeks the low heavy damp clouds had chilled the countryside as the people eagerly awaited the snowfall which would blanket the entire land until spring. Elk and red squirrels, whose homes were almost on the doorsteps of city and village dwellings, prepared for the long season. In the north and east, lynx, marten, bear, wolf, and wolverine had retreated to their dens. The season would last until sometime in April with temperatures remaining well below zero. There would be only a few hours of daylight during the long winter months but the people were accustomed to that. Their forests of pine, spruce, and birch would soon be heavily ladened with snow; their 60,000 lakes would be hard frozen to great depths; along the southern coastline, where numberless narrow, rocky and tree-clad promontories were washed by the Finnish Gulf, ice would become as strong as granite.

In November, 1939, Finns were not concerned about the coming winter. They were, however, deeply worried about what the Russians were up to. After twenty-one years of precarious independence, relations with their mammoth neighbor had deteriorated to a frustrating war of nerves. The Russians were irritated that Finland had rejected communism in favor of association with the other Scandinavian countries of Norway, Sweden, and Denmark in the Oslo Group, and that with them she had proclaimed her neutrality. These countries were convinced that common defense measures would not be necessary, even in the face of the swift war preparations building up all around them.

There had been the rebirth of the German air force and the reintroduction of conscription by Hitler. The Italian attack on Ethiopia could have been prevented had Great Britain and France been wholehearted in their opposition and well equipped to apply sanctions. And then there was the matter of Poland. The British prime minister, Neville Chamberlain, by giving a guarantee of aid to Poland if she were attacked and then being unable to fulfill his commitment because of the sheer facts of geography, had handed Russia the key to the success of both Western and German policies. France and Britain could not aid Poland without Russian help. Germany could destroy Poland with perfect security, if she had Russian consent. Whichever way Russia inclined, it could not benefit the Finns.

The nonaggression pact between Hitler and Stalin of August, 1939, was a warning so plain that it might have been written in the sky. The two countries would carve up Poland as they had intended to do ever since the Treaty of Versailles. Russia would be given license to absorb the Baltic states and Hitler could launch his first campaign undisturbed. The Western powers could neither stop nor check him.

Estonia, Latvia, and Lithuania were forced to accept treaties preparing them for outright annexation by the Soviets; in September, when war broke out between Britain and Germany, the Russians set up air and naval bases in those countries. Stalin was apparently saving Finland for last because that republic might prove more difficult to deal with. For one thing, there was the ten-year nonaggression pact signed in 1934 by Russia and Finland that had five years left to run. Many Finns counted on this agreement to save them, even though Stalin announced in the autumn of 1939: "I can well understand that you in Finland wish to remain neutral but I can assure you that this is not possible. The great powers simply will not allow it."

Finnish nerves were further frayed by a barrage of insulting Russian propaganda broadcasts, newspaper stories, and speeches. Less than 200 miles east of Helsinki, A. A. Zhdanov, the commissar of Leningrad, publicly consoled his "nervous" audience: "We people of Leningrad sit at our windows looking out at the world. Right around us lie small countries, who dream of great adventures or permit great adventurers to scheme within their borders. We are not afraid of these small nations. . . . We may feel forced to open our window a bit wider . . . call upon our Red Army to defend our country. . . ."

About this time the Finns began receiving radio broadcasts from "Moscow Tiltu," a Communist Finn who had fled to Russia when the Reds lost out in the 1918 civil war. Her programs were broadcast around the clock and contained all the news from *Pravda* and *Izvestia,* as well as editorial tidbits from the Kremlin. When she wasn't talking, she played records of the Soviet army chorus singing old Russian folk songs: "Kalinka," "Beryozomka," "Ei Ukhnem" and, for variety, bits of Brahms and Bach. The Finns loved the music but were disgusted when she interrupted their favorites with "friendly" announcements. Tiltu routinely referred to the "warmongering Tanner-Mannerheim gang," meaning Väinö Tanner, Finland's finance minister (later to become foreign minister), and Field Marshal Mannerheim. Among epithets applied to Finnish Prime Minister A. K. Cajander were "clown, crowing rooster, squirming grass snake, marionette" and "small beast of prey without sharp teeth and strength, but having a cunning lust." Cajander was accused of "standing on his head, talking upside down, smearing crocodile tears over his dirty face and weeping the repulsive tears of a clown imitating a crocodile." The Finns found such vituperation against their prime minister shocking and worrisome, but typical. Of more serious concern was the editorial in *Pravda* on November 3 which stated: "We are going to follow our own road, regardless of where it may lead. We will see to it that the Soviet Union and its borders will be protected, breaking all obstacles, in order to reach our goal."

Negotiations between the two countries actually began on April 14, 1938, when the then foreign minister of Finland, Rudolf Holsti, was approached unofficially by Boris Yartsev, a second secretary to the Russian legation in Helsinki. Yartsev had been around town for several years and had made various contacts and some friends. He was pleasant enough when necessary and, because he was not in the position of high rank, was easy to talk with. Yartsev represented the GPU, the Soviet Secret Police, and he, along with his wife, who represented a Russian travel bureau, had gotten along unusually well in the Helsinki social world, particularly with the far left group. Nevertheless, Holsti was surprised that an official call requesting an appointment would come from a second secretary rather than the Soviet Minister.

At the secret meeting between the two men Yartsev explained that while he was in Moscow two weeks ago, he had been given the authority to discuss the matter of improving relationships between the Soviet Union and Finland. He further indicated that although the USSR wished to honor Finnish independence, the leaders in Moscow were convinced that Germany was entertaining the idea of an attack against Russia. If Germany launched her attack from Finnish territory, the Soviet Union would be extremely displeased. As later reported by Väinö Tanner in his memoirs, Yartsev made it clear that in such an event, Russia would move as far as possible into Finland and the main battle would most likely be fought on Finnish soil. "Now," said Yartsev, "if Finland were to oppose the German army, Russia would help Finland with all possible economic and military assistance."

Holsti explained politely that he was in no position to make any decisions about the matter until he received instructions from his government. He then asked, "Would the Soviet Union send military forces against Finland, should Germany attack this country?"

"Yes, if Finland were not fighting alongside Russia."

Two months went by; nothing came of the talk between Yartsev and Holsti. Later it was learned that the Russian, in spite of the implied secrecy, had discussed the same matter with other key people in Helsinki, including General Aarne Sihvo and Mrs. Hella Wuolijoki, a prominent leftist Finn. He had also approached Prime Minister Cajander several times to discuss Germany's actions toward Finland and Russia. Finally the Finnish government sent a written notice to the Soviet Union. The Finnish position was that she would not allow any foreign troops on her territory, and that Finland trusted that the Soviet Union would also respect the sovereignty of her independence.

Russia's reply to the Finns' note was a proposal. Moscow suggested that if Finland would consent to a military agreement with Russia, the Soviets would be satisfied with a written promise that Finland would oppose any attack from a foreign country. The joker here, of course, was that Finland was to accept help from Russia, should an attack occur.

Moscow also wanted to increase the military strength of the Åland Islands, offshore from Turku, for the protection of Finland and Leningrad. Russia would participate by providing arms and observers to follow the work itself. Moscow further asked Finland's permission to build air and navy bases at Suursaari, a bare 70 miles east of Helsinki.

The Finnish government's reaction to these proposals was a firm "no." It was in direct opposition to the Finnish policy of neutrality to which she, together with the other Scandinavian countries, was committed.

With this kind of rejection, the Soviet press began further heated attacks on the Finns. Moscow Tiltu found more abusive phrases to sandwich in between the Red Army band and the London Philharmonic. It was during this period that Maxim Litvinov was replaced by Vyacheslav M. Molotov as the man with whom Finnish diplomats would deal. It was Molotov who summoned the Finnish negotiators to the Kremlin for a resumption of talks on "concrete political questions."

Juho Kusti Paasikivi, at that time Finnish minister at Stockholm, was chosen to lead the delegation to Moscow. This was wise, for Paasikivi, then approaching seventy, was a man of the ripest experience. Few Finns knew Russia and the Russians as he did, having studied at St. Petersburg and negotiated the 1920 Treaty of Tartu. His objective attitude towards the Soviet Union was unclouded either by sympathy for or hatred of communism. He firmly believed that Russia's interests in Finland were strictly strategic, rather than economic or ideological. A cheerful man of immense toughness, Paasikivi could be relied upon to hold the respect of both Finns and Russians. With him on those exhausting train trips in sub-zero weather back and forth between Helsinki and Moscow were Johan Nykopp and Colonel Aladár Paasonen.

Paasikivi's instructions left him little leeway for maneuvering. He could not lease Suursaari, on which the Russians had set their heart, but he could suggest the exchange of three small islands for a slice of Karelia. He was to sign no pact of mutual assistance and to insist on the right to fortify Åland. He was to add that every concession would have to be ratified by a five-sixth majority in the Finnish government.

At the Kremlin to meet the Finns on October 12, 1939, were Stalin in person, the bullet-headed, bespectacled Molotov, his assistant Potemkin, who bore a name famous in Russian history, and by Derevyanski, the minister to Helsinki of whom Yartsev had been so scornful. The meeting with this formidable array of personalities was scheduled for 5:00 P.M. Journalist-diplomat Max Jakobson later remarked in his account of these meetings: "There is a permanent Finnish-Russian agenda, and it has only one item; how to reconcile the stubborn Finnish will to independence with the Great Power ambitions of Russia."

Stalin opened the discussion with various territorial demands. He was particularly keen on Hanko, a small town on the coast west of Helsinki that he wanted to lease for thirty years as a military and naval base. He also demanded cession of certain islands in the Gulf of Finland and a frontier withdrawal of five or six miles farther west of Leningrad.

Stalin repeated his demands concerning the Finnish-Russian border on the Karelian Isthmus. In return for Finnish territories, Russia would cede an area in Soviet Karelia twice as large as the land lost to Finland. "We are asking 2,700 square kilometers," Stalin concluded, "and offer you in return 5,500. Would any other great power do that? No. Only we are that stupid."

The meeting ended with Paasikivi's decision that he must return to Helsinki to consult with his government. The Russians met again with the Finnish delegation at 9:30 that evening to present a written memorandum of their proposals.

The Finnish answer to these demands was that no mutual military aid pacts could be signed with any country, including Russia. Furthermore, Paasikivi informed Stalin he could not discuss such demands without consulting his government.

Two days later another meeting took place where Paasikivi presented his counterproposals, but Stalin was not interested. The Russians again insisted that the Finno-Russian border was too close to Leningrad and that it should be about 45 miles from that city instead of the present 20.

Said Paasikivi, "The new border your military leaders suggest is utterly impossible from an economic point of view."

Stalin's reply was, "Soldiers do not think in those terms. The mouth of the Finnish Gulf must be closed to prevent any nation from entering there. This is why the various islands and military bases at Hanko are included in our proposal."

Paasikivi asked, "Who would attack Russia?"

"It could be Germany or England." The Russian leader then referred to the nonaggression pact. "Regardless of the fact that we still have good relations with Germany, things do change in this world."

The Finns made a second trip in Moscow, arriving on October 23 and this time Väinö Tanner, who would shortly become foreign minister, was among the negotiators. At the Kremlin the story ran essentially the same as before. Hanko, as a base for the Soviets, would be out of the question; it would conflict with Finland's neutrality. The negotiators also made their formal protest about Russian military aircraft overflying their country but Stalin and Molotov ignored this. After two hours the stalemated meeting was closed. Väinö Tanner later recalled the scene in his memoirs. Molotov had looked drawn, dismayed, and surprised at the audacity of the Finns. "Are you trying to create a conflict?" he had asked Paasikivi.

The older man answered, "We don't want it, but you seem to be working toward that."

Tanner remembers Stalin smiling with his mouth, but not his eyes. It was not a comfortable game to be playing.

The negotiators left for the legation, planning to return to Finland the following night. That same evening at 9:00 a telephone message came from Molotov's secretary instructing the men to meet again at the Kremlin at 10:30. Again there would be the ashen gray faces of Russians who were on call day and night but who usually worked their hardest in the wee hours and seldom saw the sun or daylight. "Here comes our ultimatum," Tanner said.

Stalin and Molotov began the discussion as if it had never been broken off. "As far as the number of troops at Hanko is concerned, we could reduce them to 4,000," Molotov said.

"But we could not change the Karelian Isthmus border," Paasikivi retorted. "We will, however, bring these matters to our government's attention."

Paasikivi and Tanner went back to the Finnish Legation to draft a cable to Helsinki asking for instructions; their meeting ended at 2:00 A.M.

When the second discussion ended with no agreement in sight, Paasikivi remarked to his colleague, "What is the use of neutrality and Scandinavian cooperation? Our geographical position ties us to Russia. Now we must choose between a war which might turn Finland into a Bolshevik state, or submitting to life within the Soviet sphere of influence, in which case internal independence might be preserved as it was in the nineteenth century."

Tanner, for his part, wrote a letter to Per Albin Hansson, the Swedish prime minister, who was an old friend and fellow Social Democrat, asking him to make up his mind once and for all whether Finland could rely on active military help from Stockholm. He pointed out that Hanko seemed the rock upon which everything would founder, and about Hanko there could be no compromise; a lease must be refused. The answer from Hansson came quickly: "You must not in your calculations count on Swedish intervention, for it would split the Cabinet. Personally I would like to do much more, but I have to deal with a nation that is selfish about peace."

Meanwhile the Russians were losing patience. They felt they had shown proper respect for Finnish national pride and soon it would be time to take military action. By the end of October as the negotiators were about to leave for their third and last trip to Moscow, Molotov revealed to the Supreme Soviet the full extent of Russian demands, his speech being reported to the world at large. "From whom does Finland hope to get help?" the Leningrad delegate had asked. "Poland too had a guarantee."

It had now become impossible for Russia to compromise without loss of face and the Finns seriously considered breaking off their journey. On further thought, they decided to continue on the barest hope that concessions could be made.

As expected, the meeting on November 3 ended in a stalemate and as the men dispersed, Molotov said, "We civilians can't seem to do any more. Now it seems to be up to the military. It is their turn to speak."

The following day the Finns received a telephone message stating that the Russians wanted them to appear at the Kremlin at 6:00 P.M. Said Stalin: "The Soviet government is the only government that could tolerate an independent Finland. The czarist government could not tolerate it, nor could the Kerenski government. But the Soviet government demands that its borders be protected. For this reason the problem of the Finnish Gulf is important. The Soviet government will not dispose of its feelings on Hanko."

Molotov added, "Finland could legally call Hanko a concession, a rental, an exchange, a trade . . . anything she wants to."

"I am afraid Hanko cannot be given up under any circumstances," said Paasikivi.

Now the Finns were surprised to hear the Russians come out with further demands for various islands in the gulf east of Hanko. Pointing out several islands on the map, Stalin asked, "Do you need these?"

Paasikivi, taken aback, replied, "This is an entirely new matter and we would need instructions from Helsinki."

The discussion continued for a short while. Finally the Finns concluded: "We have, in our proposals, gone as far as we can. Where basic principals are at stake, we know what course we must follow."[2]

Yet, the meeting ended in a friendly enough manner. Stalin called out, "All the best," and Molotov said, *"Au revoir."*[3]

---

[2]In the Foreign Ministry's White Book a comparison was made as to what similar demands would have meant to the British Isles. For England, the Isle of Wight along with the Channel Islands would have been relinquished. The port of Southampton, the Orkney and Shetland islands would have been fortified by the enemy and the mainland's borders would have been moved inland from Norfolk about fifty miles, destroying most of Britain's fortifications in the process.

[3]Väinö Tanner, Olin Ulkoministerinä Talvisodan Aikana (Helsinki: Tammi, 1951), translations by the authors.

The Finns lingered in the Russian capital until November 13 and then returned home. They were met by an atmosphere of unrealistic optimism and a conviction that as long as negotiations were going on, matters between the two countries could be straightened out. People who had left Helsinki as a precautionary measure began to drift back. Foreign Minister Eljas Erkko was certain that the Russians would back down in the face of Finnish stubborness and world opinion.[4] Many people in high positions both at home and abroad expressed strong opinions about Russia's peaceful intent.

Meanwhile, in Karelia, General Meretskov was watching his time schedule very carefully. Soon he would receive the message he had been waiting for.

On Sunday afternoon, November 26, 1939, Finnish border guards at their outposts busied themselves with the usual things men do when they are waiting for something to happen. They played cards, drank coffee, listened to the radio, and cleaned and oiled their guns. They thought about their families, their wives, their children, their sweethearts and everybody talked about the fighting that lay ahead. What would it be like? Nobody could visualize a full-blown Russian attack on their borders and all agreed that the border guards would be bearing the first brunt of the mass assault.

Some of the younger men said they'd be glad to get it over with because the suspense of waiting for something to happen was worse than any fighting they'd have to do. "A Russian is a Russian, even if he is fried in butter," they joked derisively. The older men nodded, "We'll see."

At Mainila border post on the Karelian Isthmus, Matti Jokela patrolled the area of the Jäppinen bridge. On this Sunday afternoon he noticed that his relief was late. The fellow was probably still drinking coffee with the other soldiers inside the log cabin guardhouse a few hundred yards away. Maybe they were playing poker to relieve some of the monotony of watching Russian activities across the border.

He turned and began walking back towards the narrow, broken-down old stone bridge over the Rajajoki River that separated Mainila village on the Russian side from Jäppilä village on the Finnish side. Here the stream was a mere 12 feet wide, but varied considerably at other points along its border route. Beyond the bridge the road continued on up the hill to Mainila and the Russian guard buildings. Jokela had no way of knowing what kind of weaponry was over there, but on the Finnish side

---

[4]Erkko had been appointed foreign minister in December, 1938.

only infantry troops with light weapons were allowed near the border.

Suddenly the sound of a cannon shot pierced the afternoon's stillness. Jokela turned and faced the Russian side to watch and listen. Another shot rang out and the Finn then decided that the Russians were probably having target practice. Again the cannon boomed out. And again and again.

After things quieted down, Jokela dutifully went about his job of entering his observations in the log book. Then, just to make certain his entries were correct, he drew lines from three different observation posts on the Finnish side, pinpointing the firing spots to be about one and a quarter miles southeast from the point of explosions.

In Moscow Finnish Minister Yrjö-Koskinen was summoned to the Kremlin and told that shots had been fired by the Finns on the Soviet frontier post at Mainila, killing four men and wounding nine. Yrjö-Koskinen offered an investigation according to a longstanding procedure between the two countries, but it was useless. Moscow had arranged its own *casus belli*. Molotov told the Finnish minister the following day that his government no longer felt bound by the treaty of nonaggression and by the end of the month the Russians had begun operations with overwhelming numbers on land, sea, and air. Now everyone understood that Finland's people were faced with a battle for life. It seemed that there was to be a Russian version of the German blitzkrieg on Poland. It was the curtain call for the Soviet-Finnish dialogues that had lasted twenty months, ever since second secretary Boris Yartsev had first called on Rudolf Holsti in March, 1938.[5]

[5]Khrushchev, *Khrushchev Remembers* (Boston: Little, Brown and Company, 1970), p. 152, has two versions of the incident. The first has Stalin in his apartment saying, "Let's get started today." The hour of the ultimatum had already been set, and after the prescribed time had gone by Kulik was sent to supervise the bombardment of the Finnish border. The group learned by telephone that the salvo had been fired.

The other version is that "the Finns started shooting first and we were compelled to shoot back. It's always like that when people start a war. There was once a ritual which you sometimes see in operas; someone throws down a glove to challenge someone else to a duel; if the glove is picked up, it means the challenge is accepted. But in our time it's not always so clear-cut who starts a war."

2 NOVEMBER 30, 1939: "OUR BORDERS ARE BURNING!"

At 7:57 A.M. the Karelian fields and forests celebrated in the symphonic poems of Jean Sibelius slumbered in the frozen dark silence of winter. Overhead an airplane was flying and the Finns knew it was not one of theirs. Throughout the night soldiers had clustered around radios listening for the news because at 0045, border guards had learned that Russia had broken the nonaggression pact.

The waiting was over. They were at war.

On the stroke of 8:00 A.M. the air was suddenly filled with the whistle of shells, the echo of their detonation, the deeper boom of the howitzers and the muffled roar of the heavies. From Kronstadt, the Russian fortifications near the sea, came the distant echo of the great fortress guns. Thirty seconds later the horizon became a sheet of flame. The entire Finnish frontier was ablaze. Snow-ladened trees flew through the air; boulders, dirt, slush and bits of farmhouses were silhouetted against the deep blue-red sky of dawn. Winding country roads disappeared in chunks as if the earth had cracked and swallowed them up.

Then began the rattle of machine guns, answered by those of the Finns. The chorus was quickly identified by both sides with the Finns' rapid-fire Lahti-Saloranta automatic rifles and the Russians' slower-firing light machine guns. The cannonade continued for thirty minutes along the front which was 90 miles long and 11 miles deep. Green rockets shot up into the cold winter sky, signaling the Red infantry to attack, and the troops charged, screaming their battle cry, *"Urra!"* Plunging into the icy waters of the Rajajoki River, they immediately began work on their pontoon

15

bridges. At 9:15 sections of the first battalion crossed the frontier and over the bridges to enter Finnish Karelia.

Further north, the forests so silent an hour before the attack were suddenly filled with the roar of tank motors, the clank of treads, and the sirens of the machines along the snow-covered roads. As the fields and forests shook with exploding bomb and shell, Finns along the 800-mile-long border found themselves being attacked from every road. Even at the tiny village of Myllyjärvi to which leads only a narrow path, a strong Russian unit covered by artillery rushed across the border. Trees cracked and crashed into the deep snow sending clouds of white ice and slush, black rocks and debris mushrooming into the air. Overhead, airplanes roared low over the treetops, spraying machine-gun fire and dropping bombs. There was no nightmare with which the Finns could compare the scene. Nothing in their memories or wildest imaginations had prepared them for this.

In the beginning there were an estimated 600,000 Soviet troops in the four Russian armies; the 7th, 8th, the 9th, and the 14th striking Finland all the way from the Karelian Isthmus to Petsamo in the north. There were five invasion routes; the 9th Army was to cut Finland in half at her waistline. As the huge tanks clattered along the narrow icy roads, blasting their guns at the meager contingents of border guards, hordes of troops trudged in tight formation behind them. One Finn, wide-eyed with horror, managed to quip, "So many Russians—where will we bury them all?" His buddies laughed grimly as they noted their bullets bouncing harmlessly off the oncoming tanks.

North of Lake Ladoga the Finns went through their so-called withdrawal phase in essentially the same way that those on the Isthmus did: fight, delay, and retreat to their small trenches and fortifications in the wilderness. Here in the north there was nothing like the "luxury" of the Mannerheim Line; the men were on skis and they were experts at navigation and quite at home in temperatures of 50 degrees below zero. Nearly all were Home Guards and reservists who had grown up together, gone to school and training together, and were fine physical specimens. They knew what they were defending—their homes and farms—and their fighting was fierce, determined, almost fanatic. They were shrewd hunters and sharpshooters and no one needed to tell them when to pull the trigger or in which direction to aim.

Guerrilla fighting began in earnest almost from the moment of the

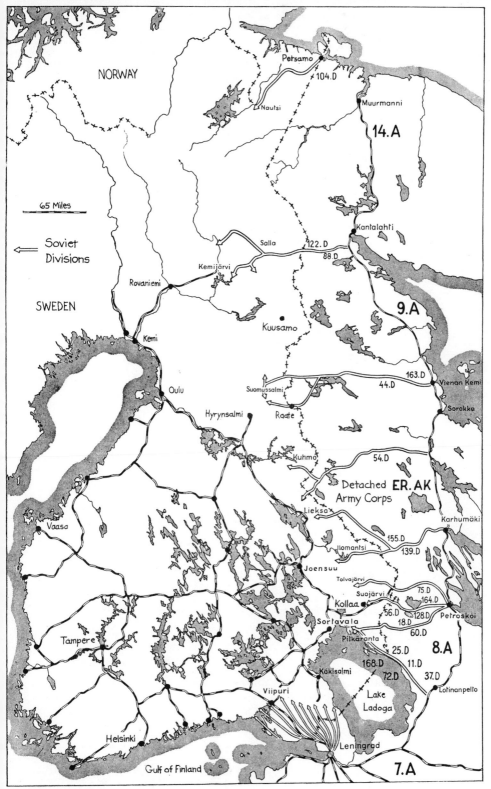

The concentration of Russian Divisions against Finland in November, 1939 *Courtesy: Werner Söderström Oy, Helsinki*

"So many Russians. Where will we bury them all?"
Cartoonist: JUSSI AARNIO. *Used by permission, Oy Lehmus, Tampere, Finland.*

Russian onslaught as white-clad ski patrols raced up and down the tracks, harassing the enemy columns. Most of these northerners had their own homemade cross-country skis with leather toe-bindings. Their handmade *pieksu,* boots with turned-up toes, fitted neatly into the toe bindings so that they could be in and out of their skis in seconds. When they crawled along the snow, shooting, they had their skis beside them attached to a leather belt.[1]

Using their quick-firing Suomi submachine guns, the skiers appeared out of nowhere, poured a deluge of bullets into the Russian masses, and then disappeared into the whiteness again.

[1]Regular ski troopers were provided with factory-made skis, bindings, and heavy-soled boots with quick-release devices.

At Petsamo in Arctic Finland the Soviet 104th and 52d divisions, supported by the coastal artillery guns of their Arctic Ocean ports, began garnering a harvest of towns, villages, and industrial property. Their plan was to push through to Rovaniemi in Lapland by December 12 and they expected little opposition from the local forces. The odds here were forty-two Russians against each defending Finn.

At the Salla-Savukoski area, a doubleheaded spear of the Russian 88th Division together with the 122d rumbled into the small Lapland village of Salla, anticipating a quick victory and a reunion with the forces from Petsamo at Rovaniemi.

Seventy miles south of Salla, at Kuusamo, Finland's "Switzerland," with its vast snow-covered fells and frozen lakes, the Finns left a few guards to protect the road that led to Rovaniemi, but when no mass attack occurred, these men skied south to join the defenders of Suomussalmi.

Suomussalmi was Finland's waistline, the shortest distance to Oulu and an area where the Murmansk railroad could bring supplies to the Red Army. Moreover, the road system on the Finnish side was good, and as the troops stormed over the border, they brought their own heavy road-building equipment, along with tanks, trucks, artillery, horses, field kitchens, propaganda leaflets, gifts, brass bands, and the troops of the 163d Division, some 17,000 strong.

Meanwhile, civilians were being evacuated as quickly as possible. Some made it to Norway or to safety in the interior countryside. Others were not so fortunate. At Kuhmo, 65 miles south of Suomussalmi, border guards Kimpimäki and Tauriainen skied towards the farmhouse known as Laamasenvaara, about 2.5 miles from the main road, to arrange for the family's evacuation. "The Russians are coming," they announced. "You'll have to leave!"

"But first would you have coffee?" the guards were asked.

"*Kiitos*, thank you." They would have hot coffee to thaw their chilled bones and they would have *reikäleipä*, dark bread which was strung along a pole across the top of the huge fireplace. The guards hung their fur caps on the reindeer antlers in the front hall and went in to sit before the fire.

Suddenly there was a pounding on the door. It burst open and a half-dozen Russians came at them. Tauriainen grabbed his rifle and hit the first man on the head with the rifle butt. Now the comrades backed off into the entrance hall and began throwing hand grenades into the living room. The Finn guards quickly scooped them up and threw them back. There were explosions and gunfire with one fatal bullet hitting the little boy who was sitting on his mother's knee at the coffee table. The two Finnish guards leaped through the back window, hoping to make it back to their forces to give warning, but they were caught in the courtyard and killed.[2]

At Kuhmo the Russian 54th Division led by Major General Gusevski advanced along the Repola-Hukkajärvi road with 12,800 men, more than 120 artillery pieces, and 35 tanks. Finnish Lieutenant Kaariala's 1,200 reservists attacked and counterattacked before withdrawing from the uneven battle.

Elsewhere on the northern frontier, the Russian 139th Division rumbled along all available roads leading to Tolvajärvi, a 10-mile long frozen lake with its little village, church, and co-op store. The 20,000 Reds led by General Beljajev brought with them some 147 artillery pieces and 45 panzers which they would use against 4,200 home-town Finns.

Reserve Lieutenant Toiviainen was celebrating his forty-fifth birthday that morning at the border post near Artahuhta. His men had come to congratulate him and present him with a new pen. The commander had just made his thank-you speech when sounds of heavy guns echoed from the direction of Myllyjärvi. The men's silent awe was finally broken by Toiviainen saying, "Comrade Molotov must have ordered gunfire in my honor. Let's get going!"

Toiviainen with his group of cavalrymen galloped to join Myllyjärvi's fifteen defending guards but they were unable to stop the onslaught. Retreating to Artahuhta, they found themselves confronted with solid rows of Russian machine guns. The fire was deadly with troops often separated by only a few yards. One cavalryman sneaked behind the enemy lines, killed a machine gunner, took his place, and fired the weapon at the Russians the entire night before his deception was discovered. Bullet wounds paralyzed his left arm as he miraculously escaped to his own side. He solved his dilemma by holding the rifle against his knee and chest to load it, then resting it on a firm platform to fire.

Artahuhta held for two days and two nights before a retreat to another defense position was ordered.

Most civilians living in villages and farms along the border had been evacuated earlier, particularly after the Mainila shots four days before. A tragic exception was Hyrsylä, a point of Finnish land surrounded on three

---

[2]The family was taken to Russia as prisoners. They later returned to find the ruins of their home.

sides by Soviet territory, where the people refused to take the war seriously. Besides, they had been reassured by the Home Guard that they would not be forgotten should real trouble break out. Now suddenly they saw their neighbors' houses burning and they realized that in the haste and confusion of the fighting they had been completely cut off by the advancing Reds. Several villages along with more than 1,000 people were taken over. Only ten civilians managed to make their way through the forests to the west. Taken prisoner was Matti Pajunen, retired elementary school teacher and head of the Hyrsylä Home Guard,[3] and the many Lottas,[4] women auxilliaries. Sheep and cows were left by the wayside to freeze to death and all property was destroyed, either by the departing Finns or the oncoming Russians.

At Lieksa further north, 6,400 Russians with 40 artillery cannon and 12 tanks screamed *"Urra!"* as they attacked the Finns' 12th and 13th Detached Battalions with their combined manpower of 3,200 and four artillery cannon.

Isolated as they were, the men of the north had no idea what was going on in the Karelian Isthmus; what was more, small ski patrol units seldom saw each other as they set out on their individual assignments. It would be some time before these Finns who loved their solitude would get used to such traffic in their country.

[3]Matti Pajunen and many others from Hyrsylä were returned after the war in a prisoner exchange.

[4]*Lottas* date back to the 1808–09 war between Russia and Sweden when a young Finnish officer took his wife along with him to the front. Her name was *Lotta* and she endeared herself to the troops by cooking, nursing, writing letters for the wounded and doing all manner of chores for them. *Lottas* served during the War of Independence, the Winter War and throughout World War II.

3 | HELSINKI AFLAME

For the people of Helsinki, Thursday, November 30, 1939, began quite normally. It was one more day in the war of nerves and many civilians had forced themselves into a state of numbness to it all. Everyone knew that Russia had broken off diplomatic relations and that almost anything could happen at any time. But life and work must go on, regardless.

The weather was brisk and clear for the first time in a week. The streets were filled with early shoppers and people hurrying about their jobs.

Then, without warning, at 9:25 A.M. air-raid sirens shrieked. Startled pedestrians looked up to see Russian airplanes dropping Finnish-language leaflets. No one was sure what else might be falling their way as they scurried to the shelter of cellars and parks. There was no panic, only shocked disbelief that this was actually happening to them.

Later, when the all clear was sounded, the Finns read what the Soviet government had to say: "You know we have bread—don't starve. Soviet Russia will not harm the Finnish people. Their disaster is due to their wrong leadership. Mannerheim and Cajander must go. After that, peace will come."

At 2:30 that afternoon more Russian bombers roared out of the sky. In three shattering bombardments they rained incendiary bombs on the dazed population. Buildings collapsed and fires raged through the city. The afternoon attack caught the busy street traffic and pedestrians, and it was estimated that 200 were killed in the explosions or were buried in the rubble of falling buildings. The Russian bombers had apparently aimed their projectiles at the railroad station, the harbor, and the airport, but it was soon learned that the bombardiers' aim was far from accurate.

Clouds of smoke hid the treetops as civil defense workers tried to put out blazes and dug through the rubble for injured persons and those who had been killed.

At least fifty bombs fell in the Frederiksgatan; the big technical high school was totally demolished. Several five- and six-story apartment houses in the neighborhood were destroyed; glass splinters, stones, and debris littered the roads. Automobiles were in flames and everywhere was the smell of burning flesh, the cries of the injured. At the railroad station, where thousands of city residents sought transportation into the countryside and supposed safety, there was terrible confusion. There was no need for the people of Helsinki to carry out their carefully rehearsed

The first air-raid siren. Mari asks, "Does that siren concern civilians too?"
Cartoonist: JUSSI AARNIO. Published in Korven Kaiku. *Used by permission, Oy Lehmus, Tampere, Finland.*

blackout against air raids; the blazing skyline was visible for miles.

Finland's little air force did what it could that infamous day. But there was small chance for them to show much, save heart. Nevertheless, during the last days of November, all Finnish pilots had been ordered to full combat readiness. The Mercury engines of the Fokkers had been tested and tuned to perfection. Machine guns were checked and rechecked, ammunition belts were loaded, parachutes repacked, and all pilots along with their maintenance personnel stood by in full readiness.

At Immola Air Base near the vital Imatra power station, some 30 miles north of Viipuri, the 24th Fighter Squadron stood by with its eight Fokker D-fighters, three commissioned, and five noncommissioned pilots. During the last several days the younger, less experienced pilots had received additional training, particularly in the air-to-air and air-to-ground gunnery practice. When not in the air, the duty period was passed in the ready tent where a portable gramophone played the latest Finnish hit songs and the men talked about the war news.

In the early morning hours of November 30 Captain Eino Luukkanen and the other pilots were playing poker. Luukkanen had been having an exceptionally good run of hands and had just been dealt perfect cards when Colonel Riku Lorentz ran up to the front of the ready tent, fired a shot in the air with his service revolver, and shouted, "This is it, men! This morning at 0615 hours Russian forces crossed our borders." Now, reports came in that several Russian bombers were approaching Viipuri. Luukkanen grabbed his flight helmet and raced for the door. His mechanic was already winding the starter. Luukkanen climbed onto the wing of his Fokker and lowered himself into the cockpit. Within five minutes he and three other pilots in their aircraft were heading for Viipuri. Luukkanen was leading the first actual combat flight of the Winter War.

Flying just beneath the cloud base at 2,000 feet, cruising at 186 miles per hour, the squadron would make its destination in twenty minutes. But twenty minutes was ample time for the enemy bombers to make their run and turn for home. At 0945 hours the familiar old city appeared below. To starboard Luukkanen could see that his fears were well founded; several buildings at Maaskola railroad yards were already in flames. The Russians had dropped their bombs and departed.

Luukkanen veered southward and spotted two of the Soviet bombers disappearing into the clouds over Uuraa. The Finns climbed above the cloud layer into sunshine at 5,000 feet but there was no sign of the enemy. After about an hour of patrolling the area without seeing another aircraft except three of their own Bulldogs, the disappointed Finns headed for home base. Flying through heavy snow clouds which were thickening as they neared Immola, they were forced finally to fly at virtually treetop level. At the base they learned that Viipuri had been bombed at 0942 hours, just three minutes before their arrival.

It was frustrating and maddening. But tomorrow was another day. There would be plenty of chances to tangle with the Soviet air force.[1]

The two navies were in action that day as the Russians took over some of the undefended islands off the southern coast. Also the Russian cruiser *Kirov* and two destroyers fired on the Russarö fortress near Hanko. In the short battle one destroyer was damaged and left the formation but there were no casualties on the coast. Finland's two 4,000-ton armored ships, the *Väinämöinen* and *Ilmarinen*, each equipped with eight 40-mm. and eight 105-mm. guns steamed into Turku waters to set up their anti-aircraft artillery defense of that vital port. Finland's five submarines, the *Ikuturso*, *Vesihiisi*, and *Vetehinen* of the 500-ton class and the *Vesikko*, 250 tons, and *Saukko*, 99 tons, began patrolling the Gulf of Finland all the way to the Gulf of Riga in Latvia, harassing Russian ship movements and carrying out reconnaissance assignments. Also in operation were the two 450-ton gunboats, the *Uusimaa* and *Hämeenmaa*, and the two 370-ton *Karjala* and *Turunmaa*, along with ten 15-ton motor torpedo boats.

The 13,000 men in the Finnish navy, commanded by Major General V. Valve, would, when the seas froze, form a special group the size of two battalions of infantry and call themselves "Battalion Aaltonen."

In Helsinki, as well as Viipuri, Hanko, Kotka, and other cities where bombs fell, the Finnish anti-aircraft batteries went into action. Several bombers were shot down but this gave little comfort to the defenders. There were hundreds more where those came from. With the Red Army pushing into the Karelian Isthmus, as well as other points north of Ladoga, all the way to Petsamo, Finnish President Kyösti Kallio proclaimed a "state of war."

It was almost the bleakest day in the young republic's history.

As machine guns strafed the city streets, the Finnish government moved its headquarters from the parliament building in Helsinki to a

[1] This account is based on events related in *Fighter over Finland* by Eino Luukkanen (London: Macdonald and Company, 1963).

more protected area in the outskirts. That night parliament, in a secret meeting, gave the Cajander government a vote of confidence, but the prime minister and his cabinet resigned in the hope that a new government might work more amicably with the Russians. The new government, headed by Risto Ryti, governor of the Bank of Finland, immediately announced its intention to seek peace. However, even though Ryti was ready to negotiate, he said: ". . . We will not consent to bargain away our independence."

Meanwhile from "somewhere in Finland," an unknown radio station announced that the Finnish Communist Party had set up a "democratic government of Finland" with Comrade Otto Kuusinen at its head. This puppet government had its headquarters at Terijoki, the first town to be "liberated" by the Red Army. In reality, Terijoki, a beach resort on the Gulf of Finland a few miles from the Soviet-Finnish border, had been abandoned by the frontier guards without a fight. The Soviet government immediately entered into diplomatic relations with the Kuusinen government. Molotov must have enjoyed his talks with Kuusinen, a Marxist Finn, because in one day he succeeded in persuading the head of the new "people's government" to lease the Hanko peninsula, to cede a slice of territory on the Karelian Isthmus, and to sell an island in the Gulf of Finland, along with Finnish sections of the Fisherman's peninsula for a sum of 300 million finnmarks. Kuusinen, a leader of the Red insurrection during the civil war, had fled to Russia at the time of the White Finn victory, and conjecture was that he never left Russia until the Kremlin set him up in business in Terijoki.[2]

The reaction of the Finns was the complete opposite of what the Soviets had hoped. Not only was the puppet government the laughing stock of the world, but it united the Finns even more closely. This ridiculous ploy gave the Finns no choice but to fight, if they wished to continue to exist as an independent democratic state.

[2]Today, the resort town of Terijoki bears the Russian name Zelenogorsk. Finnish writer Esko J. Mannermaa, in New World, August, 1969, doubts that Kuusinen had set up his government by December 1 because only the day before, the Red Army was fighting its first battles twenty miles to the east. Kuusinen could not have reached the town until later—except on paper.

In Terijoki there was no local populace to be appointed as "Cabinet members," because everyone had been evacuated to the west. Consequently, the entire cabinet was made up of Soviet citizens, leftist Finns who had fled to the USSR after the civil war.

4 MARSHAL MANNERHEIM AND THE "BLITZ" AT THE KARELIAN ISTHMUS

At the Karelian Isthmus, where the Russians' 7th Army with nine divisions poured over the border, there was mass confusion on both sides. As Soviet artillery bombarded from the southeast and shells exploded in the flaming sky, thousands of Finnish refugees with their cows, horses, wagons, sleighs, children, and old folks clogged the roads that the Finnish army was using to get to the front. The narrow country roads could just barely accomodate single-lane traffic, so that any passing had to be done on a stand-aside basis.

For the Russians, it was bumper-to-bumper traffic and hopeless jams along the jigsaw-puzzle roads as vehicles got stuck in ditches or were otherwise disabled. In the midst of all this, a heavy snowfall stopped all traffic, and it was several days before the Reds could jockey their artillery into positions where they could fire effectively. The snowfall helped the Finnish refugees because it grounded the Soviet planes, but when the skies cleared, aircraft bombed and strafed the hapless people as they made their way through the snow.

Soviet heavy tanks trying to cross through the swamplands added to the muddle. Where the ice had not frozen solid, panzers simply disappeared beneath the cracked ice and snow. Minefields and demolitions guarded every avenue of approach. The Russians tripped treacherous threads and wires across the roads, connected with explosives. If they opened a barn door, crossed a threshold, or set foot on a bridge, they detonated the traps. If a Red soldier kicked at a dead pig, it exploded, or if he tried on a white fur cape, that too blew up. Even if he prodded a pile of manure, he instantly learned that it had been mined by the "fiendish" Finns.

Nikolai Virta wrote for *Pravda*: "What cads! They [the Finns] can't fight and break their heads running from us, but how well they make such nastiness. They are masters of foul play. . . . When our tired men wanted to drink, they found all the village wells filled with earth. Our enemies are perfidious, cowardly and are filled with base and tricky cunning. Hardly had the first Red fighter set foot on Finnish soil when an explosion rent the air. Mines are everywhere. Moving along the Viipuri road toward the village of Jäppinen, from which the Finns had just been driven, we saw it burning, set on fire by the Finns." The Soviet writer explained that when the Russian troops tried to fill the ditches dug by the Finns as tank traps, the first shovelful of dirt detonated a mine. "On every path and every road there is invisibile danger prepared by a vicious and barbarious band. Before our eyes, mines burst under tanks, they burst under heaps of manure and hay stacks or beneath snow banks."

Near the border on the Finnish side where the mined sectors were the tightest, the Finns saw Soviet troops advancing hand in hand, singing amid the screams of mangled men, paying no attention to exploding mines and Finnish snipers. Loaded down as they were with propaganda leaflets, gifts, money, and clothing for the Finnish populace they were to liberate, and followed closely by their *Politruks* (political commissars) who would shoot them if they turned back, they had little choice but to continue their forward movement. Adding to the oddity of this military invasion was the obvious fact that neither side really knew what the other was doing. Intelligence reports concerning the capability and tactical plans for offense and defense were almost immediately obsolete; prewar tactics that had been taught from military manuals quickly became useless within a day or so after the attack began.

Headlines around the world told of the "Finns on the Run" and claimed that the Russians had made great gains. But the reporters were filing their stories from Hotel Kamp in Helsinki. Marshal Mannerheim would not allow them to go to the front because ". . . This is war, not Hollywood." Few Western reporters could speak Finnish or Russian, let alone ski over the vast country in sub-zero temperatures. So they had to be content with the fragmentary, though basically honest reports they got from the Finns. They left the rest to their creative imaginations.

As for Russian reporting, it was good news, or none, or masterpieces of fiction. One Soviet newspaper complained that sharpshooters of Finland's white-clad ski units were resorting to the use of "bandit tactics" in sudden attacks on Russian columns. "The enemy does not engage in open battle. Hidden under white robes and thus skillfully camouflaged, they suddenly dart from the woods to fire at our advancing units. Then in all haste they run, frequently taking off their boots to ski only in their stockings."

At his headquarters in the elementary school in Mikkeli, 85 miles northwest of Viipuri, Field Marshal Carl Gustav Mannerheim, supreme commander of Finland's Defense Forces, concerned himself only briefly with what the newspapers had to say about the attack on Finland. It came as no surprise because for years, in his position as chairman of the Defense Council, he had warned his government of Russia's reviving potentialities. He had had no faith in collective security for the protection of small countries but each request he had made for improving national defense had been met with indifference. He had been repeatedly asked, "What is the use of spending so much money on the armed forces when there won't be any war?"

In utter frustration, he had decided to resign his position in 1937, since ". . . My work has been thankless and the ideas I had initiated had not gained sufficient support from either the president or the government." Only repeated urgings of Kyösti Kallio, the new president, persuaded him to stay. In the summer of 1939 Prime Minister A. K. Cajander was prepared to accept Mannerheim's resignation and had begun to search for a new chairman of the Defense Council. During the crucial diplomatic negotiations in the autumn of 1939, leaders of the National Coalition Party privately criticized Mannerheim as too old and too afraid of the Soviet Union and as—of all things—a man whose word could not be trusted. Only a few days before the Winter War began, President Kallio agreed in principle to Mannerheim's threatened resignation. But the war began before Mannerheim's resignation was submitted and at the age of seventy-two, he undertook the arduous task of leading the Finnish Defense Forces against the Soviet Union.

Carl Gustav Mannerheim was one of two Finns (the other being Jean Sibelius) of whom most educated Westerners had heard. An extremely complicated, sophisticated, and atypical Finn, he had never been a real nationalist. Born into a Swedish-speaking family, he never learned the Finnish language until he was past fifty and then it was only on the par with Winston Churchill's famous French pronunciations. Instead, he spoke the great cultural languages of Europe; in 1918, when he headed the White Home Guard to fight the Russians for Finnish independence, he required an interpreter to deal with his troops.

Yet, for the people of Finland, Marshal Mannerheim was the great military hero. Tall, able, and still handsome, his career was legend; he represented unity, the flag, and everything that was strong and good in Finland. School children could recite how he had served with the czar's army when Finland and Russia were on cordial terms. Few knew that he had been expelled from the Finnish Cadet Corps for disciplinary reasons, but it was general knowledge that as a young officer he had gone to Manchuria and Korea to participate in the Russo-Japanese war of 1904–05 and for years afterwards had traveled hitherto unexplored parts of Asia via Samarkand, Kashgar, the Gobi Desert, and the Silk Road. He served for six years in Poland, then a Russian possession, and during World War I he fought in the Russian Imperial Army. He married the daughter of a well-known and well-to-do Russian family, Anastasie Arapov, whose father was a general *à la suite* of the czar. He deeply and persistently loved the old Russia he grew to know during his career in the Imperial Army.

Mannerheim loathed bolshevism. When he returned to his native country to lead the White Finns against the Reds during the 1918 civil war, it was not because of any hatred for Russia. It was because he despised communism and all it stood for.

Strangely enough, Gustav Mannerheim was never *in* the Finnish army. He was, during the civil war, the commander in chief of the White Home Guard; the Finnish army was at that time nonexistent, having been abolished during the period of Russification. Constitutionally, Mannerheim's position was *above* the Finnish army. A brilliant leader during Finland's great Winter War crisis, he never accepted democracy, nor parliamentary government which was the institutional expression of Finnish democracy. He refused to join or lead any party; his leadership, when offered, was intensely personal. In this stubborn individualism, he was more Finn than "Knight of Europe," as he had often been called.

Mannerheim's aristocratic bearing had always commanded awe and respect from famous personages as well as the unknown. In August, 1939, while he was still chairman of the Defense Council, he had the dubious pleasure of reviewing some 100,000 Finnish reservists, most of whom wore their own civilian clothing and who had only recently been refreshed on their military marching instructions. The war maneuvers took place near Viipuri and among the notables who reviewed the four-hour-long

parade were Prime Minister A. K. Cajander, Swedish Defense Minister
Edvin Sköld, Finnish Minister of Defense Juho Niukkanen, and General
E. Linder. But the unfashionable array of Finnish reservists only had eyes
for their hero, Marshal Mannerheim, who sat on horseback and saluted
the men, hour after hour. Later that same day Cajander made a speech
which he later regretted. Said the prime minister of Finland, then less
than three months away from a shooting war with 180 million people:
"We are proud of the fact that we don't have a lot of weapons and rifles
rusting away in the warehouses and we don't have a lot of uniforms rotting
and mildewing in the storehouses. But we do have a high standard of
living in Finland and an educational system we can be proud of. . . ."

"Cleanliness is half the meal." The Finn soldier uses his "foot rag," which was worn in
place of socks, as a napkin.
Cartoonist: JUSSI AARNIO. Gag: JUSSI SARVA. *Used by permission, Oy Lehmus, Tampere,
Finland.*

At his headquarters Mannerheim soberly reviewed Finland's situation. Obviously the Russians had been coveting Finnish territory for some time. As far back as August, 1935, Leningrad's Commissar Zhdanov had made a trip on the Murmansk Railroad, which parallels the Finnish border from Petsamo all the way south to the Karelian Isthmus. Zhdanov had also driven by car along the roads leading from the railroad to the Finnish frontier, after which he began building railroad spur tracks which headed westward. Fifty miles of railroad had been laid near the Kuusamo and Suomussalmi area; 40 miles of track were aimed at Kuhmo and Lieksa. Even as Red troops swarmed over the border on November 30, 1939, finishing touches were being made on railroad sections near the Ladoga frontier.

There was a joker, however, and for a change it appeared advantageous to the Finns to be living in a poor country. Once the Red Army set foot on Finnish soil, they would run out of railroads until they reached the interior; good roads would be equally scarce. The trick would be to stop the enemy before he could reach these good roads and railways.

The areas about which Mannerheim was most concerned were those of Suomussalmi and Salla and the Hyrynsalmi railroad station, which would assure the enemy easy passage to Oulu 150 miles to the west. It was here, too, that Soviet agents had been working on the Finnish people for the past twenty years. In recent times their voting had indicated strong Communist leanings; Stalin and his planners would count on their past popularity for an easy victory in Suomussalmi-Salla.

Another area of concern was the Karelian Isthmus where Finnish railroads ran all the way to the Finland Station in Leningrad. Also close to Russian territory was the Suojärvi railroad, north of Lake Ladoga. Although the entire Finnish frontier was in peril, Mannerheim would consider these sectors as emergencies and send reinforcements accordingly.

But even as the Field Marshal struggled with his defense plans and sent his reserves to the critical areas, he knew that this would not be a battle-by-the-book kind of war. If anything were saved, or even a bit of time gained until help could arrive from Sweden or from the West, it would be because of the caliber of officers and men who served under him. An agonizing thought that he dared not indulge himself in was the conviction that, with sufficient weaponry and air power, this particular Finnish army could drive the Russians back to their own territory. A few years earlier, when the circumstances had been different, the idea would have been preposterous. Had the Russians chosen the early 1930s to attack, they might well have had the support of Finnish leftist workers and peasants. But by the end of the 1930s there had been a complete change in thinking. Even the lowest-paid workers and leftists had been swept up in the feeling of independence for Finland and distrust of Russia. The Soviets were either unaware of this reversal or chose to ignore it.

His officers were not only well trained militarily but were often the country's intellectuals. Most were exceptionally versatile, capable of switching from a quiet life of science or business to leadership in war. Mannerheim's chief of staff, Lieutenant General Karl Lennart Oesch, forty-seven-year-old scholarly botanist, was known for his even temperament and great interest in scientific detail. In contrast, he was also a graduate of the 27th Jaeger Battalion in 1915, the War Academy in France, and had earlier distinguished himself in the Rautu battles of the Independence War. He held a Doctor of Philosophy degree, had been director of the Finnish War Academy until 1929, and was Minister of Interior until 1932.

In the field the Northern Finland Group, responsible for a 400-mile sector stretching from Petsamo to Kuhmo, was led by Major General E. Viljo Tuompo, a farmer's son who became a history and language expert. Tuompo, a graduate of the Jaeger Battalion, was a captain during the Independence War; later he wrote a Finnish military handbook in Berlin, and graduated from the Swedish War College. Tall, slim, and hardworking, he was an expert in Finnish defense matters. His officers, most notably Colonel A. Viikla, were from Border Guard Headquarters who had made plans and trained for this war long before hostilities began. Reports reaching Mannerheim's headquarters indicated that Tuompo's forces were facing two Russian armies, the 14th and 9th from Kuollaa and Vienan Karelia.

To lead the so-called Lapland Group, Mannerheim sent, on December 13, Major General K. M. Wallenius, a Swedish-trained military expert who had fought in Lapland in 1918 and knew the country well. The job called for a man who could do wonders with small, poorly-equipped units in the northern wilderness. Even though Wallenius would be facing the Russian 104th and 52nd divisions with only four ceremonial cannon dating back to 1887 (only about one-half of the shells exploded when fired), Mannerheim hoped the Soviets could be stopped by the clever guerrilla tactics of the ski patrollers.

Commanding the 4th Army Corps, deployed from Lieksa to Sortavala, a distance of 275 miles, was Major General J. Heiskanen. Within a few days Mannerheim replaced him with Major General J. Woldemar Hägglund, an officer with an outstanding military record in the Jaeger Battalion and the civil war, who was completely familiar with the terrain north of Ladoga. Hägglund was a sturdy, dark-haired Finn, well liked by his officers and men; he would be defending Kollaa, Tolvajärvi, Ägläjärvi, and other vital points against some ten attacking Russian divisions. As events later proved, Hägglund was a brilliant choice as leader in this area.

Under Hägglund was the so-called Group T, named for and commanded by Colonel Paavo Talvela, who at forty-one could look back on a remarkable career. At twenty he had joined the Jaeger Battalion in Germany, and a year later he was a battalion commander during the civil war. After the war he became a regimental commander with the Border Guard. As a business man, he was vice president of Suomi Filmi and vice president of the State Liquor Board. In 1939, he found himself going to war again. Serving under him in Group T were two other well-known military experts, Colonel P.O. Ekholm and Lieutenant Colonel Aaro O. Pajari.

To the vital area of Suomussalmi, Mannerheim would send forty-seven-year-old Colonel Hjalmar Siilasvuo. Here again was a Jaeger Battalion officer who had fought in the Independence War as a battalion commander. The son of a newspaper editor, he had studied law, served in the Ministry of Education, and was head of the Mobilization Bureau in later years. Mannerheim knew him as a short, sturdy, blond, opinionated man who by the same token was a shrewd and wiley military leader. If anyone could stop the Russians at Suomussalmi, it would be Siilasvuo.[1]

Mannerheim was satisfied that he had ordered the right officers to the right places.

There was the question now of tactics. Mannerheim knew his own Finnish generals well; he also knew the Russians who were leading the attacks. Because of his long association with the czar's army, he could almost read the Russian mind and anticipate the Reds' strategy. He was completely familiar with the manuals from which they were taught, because he had studied them through the years. It was a strange, though fortunate, position to be in.

He pondered the wartime experience of both armies and found each

---

[1]Today, Siilasvuo's son Ensio is serving as a general with the United Nations peacekeeping forces in Jerusalem.

of them wanting in certain areas of professionalism. The Finnish army, composed mainly of hastily recruited reservists, had no applicable lessons learned from their civil war, where battles were fought along roads and near villages and buildings which gave them shelter. During that period there were no basic military rules or manuals and the training level was low; the officers, though colorful, were nevertheless strongly influenced by their Russian, Swedish, and German tactical schooling. These tactics depended on big armies and heavy weaponry, neither of which the Finns had. There was no special training in guerrilla activities, no applicable rules for Finland's unusual terrain. Mannerheim's officers and men would have to learn to fight this kind of war on the job.

In contrast to the Finns, the Russian armies had hundreds of years of inherited war experience behind them. Even the disastrous 1904–05 war with Japan had provided them with knowledge that they put to use during World War I. Unfortunately for the Red Army, this experience could not be used after the revolution; literally thousands of professional officers and soldiers of the czar's army had been liquidated.[2] The theoretical and practical leadership was not there anymore, because the Reds despised anything that was old—namely the czar and the heritage of the army. Early reports to headquarters verified Mannerheim's belief that the level of the junior officers and noncommissioned officers was indeed low.

Mannerheim had little use for what the Bolsheviks referred to as officers; to the old aristocrat, these men would always be peasants no matter how many stars they wore on their uniforms. Any tactical gains made would be the result of brute force, fanaticism, and blind obedience prompted by the *Politruks'* guns poking in the backs of every man on the field. Leadership would still be based on the old rule books no matter how insistent the Reds were that such traditions had been scrapped. Mannerheim was convinced that the Red armies would be unable to cope with Finland's frozen forests, lakes, and wilderness—at least in the beginning.

The Finnish army was a strange lot for a man of Mannerheim's background to be leading into a major war. Most of the reservists wore their own civilian clothing, with perhaps a cap or belt insignia to identify them as friend. Their marching was sloppy, their turns poorly executed, and

[2]Arrests and executions probably reached their high point at the end of 1937 or the beginning of 1938. They continued even after the "lord high executioner" himself, the head of the Soviet Secret Police, Nikolai Ivanovich Yezhov, was found floating face down in a river. He was succeeded by Lavrenty P. Beria.

they had little interest in advancing in rank. Often reservists called officers by their first names, particularly during battle situations; saluting was a matter of friendliness and convenience. But, he considered, this army still clung to the childlike faith that it had the ability to protect the country, regardless of lack of weaponry and equipment.

Mannerheim, in evaluating the two opposing forces, realized that his only hope was to position individual Finns far apart along hundreds of miles in the north. These expert skiers would be ordered to make wide circles through the wilderness, carrying their own supporting materials with them, and attack Russian columns from the sides and from the rear. They would operate with no instructions other than to keep the situation flexible and solve each problem as it appeared.

The Finns would attack without artillery preparation (since they had little capability of that anyway) and they would strike in the dark or during snowstorms and fog.

Mannerheim would group his reserves so that they could quickly counterattack and be mobile enough to be used again miles away, wherever things were going badly.

Setting up defenses in the forests would depend on the time available. Ideally the Finns would build a main defense line deep in the woods, cutting down trees as fire lanes for their guns. Given sufficient time and men, they would lay another defense line, not too far from the first; and sometimes even a third, manned by reserves. Theoretically the main force of the enemy would be engaged, while encircling patrols would be sent out to hit the enemy from the sides or from behind.

So much for theories and tactics. But Mannerheim had no idea at this point whether or not they would work. No one did.

5 RUSSIAN PANZERS— AND THE STATE LIQUOR BOARD—GO TO WAR

Lieutenant General Hugo Viktor Österman, commander of the Finnish army at the Karelian Isthmus, stamped the snow from his boots, then hung his fur hat on the rack. His face was grim as he sank into his chair beside the warming stove and accepted the cup of hot coffee his aide poured for him. Inspection of the Russian tank situation in the field revealed that matters were even worse than he, as a professional military man, had anticipated.

He himself had seen panzers before (belonging to the armies of other countries), but few of his men had ever witnessed masses of heavy panzers rumbling towards them in the snow, firing in all directions. Even the well-trained regulars who were ready to face their enemy with little or no weaponry felt a strange tingling in their spines as they heard tens of large-sized monsters with roaring engines thundering along their lines. Psychologically they represented a terrifying black cloud of doom; an unfamiliar enemy whose actions were not those of a man but an awesome, impenetrable box of death. Tanks could get across mud and snow and plunge through barbed-wire barricades. They had the armor to stop machine-gun bullets and the fire to drive the infantry from its trenches. The Finns, in their helplessness against them, shortly began to call the tanks *romurauta*, scrap iron, and *surmanloota*, death box, but this was mainly talk to cover their dread.

For the Russian foot soldier panzers meant power, protection, and a piece of Mother Russia to follow into battle. They were a comfort and morale booster to the men who would very soon begin to feel disenchant-

37

ment with fighting a winter war in Finland. As long as tanks were in action, they would divert shrapnel that would otherwise be hitting the infantry. The Red Army was convinced that their panzers would lead them to victory; Österman, noting the hasty withdrawal of his forces, conceded that the Russians might be right in this thinking.

In the beginning it seemed hopeless to overcome the tank menace and for this the Finns could blame their own government's naivety and the fact that no one seriously thought there would be an all-out war. There had been serious budget debates over whether sums should be spent for education and health matters or defense weaponry which would probably be outdated should the time come when it would be needed. In 1936 the military did suggest that anti-panzer guns be bought, but the cost would be 27 million finnmarks; the vote was in the negative and the order, which would have given the Finnish army at least six pieces of anti-panzer artillery to each battalion along with replacement stores, was canceled.

Not until 1939 when negotiations were crumbling and weapons rattling on both sides of the border did the Finns take stock of their anti-panzer situation. Their so-called elephant cannon was finally approved for the army but it was too late for it to make front-line duty. When the war started, the Finns received one or two 37-mm. panzer cannon per battalion, making a grand total 100 for the entire army.

Almost immediately Österman began receiving reports on how the tanks were operating and usually they indicated that the Russians weren't too sure of what to do with their fine equipment. Sometimes the tanks came in pairs, the medium-heavy leading the light; later they came in groups of three to ten with the first opening the road while the second tried to keep the defenders down. They fought in open fields, close to the roadside, and sometimes they moved along the front, stopping periodically to fire towards the line. Before snow began hampering their movements, they could travel up to 18 miles per hour but later, in five to eighteen inches of snow, they were slowed down to 5 miles per hour. Oddly enough, they seldom tried to get to the defenders' line but preferred to move about just in front of them. When the infantry faltered and showed lack of interest in attack, the tanks circled around and brought them back under their protective wings.

As the shock of the initial Russian attack wore off, Finnish border troops began to show their mettle. Noting that the Russians shunned the darkness, the Finns sent nightly patrols through the woods to attack the enemy campsites. Österman's border troops fired their field artillery on a straight trajectory to destroy the oncoming panzers while ski troopers hit the infantry from the sides and Finnish sharpshooters picked off the tightly clustered Red soldiers by the hundreds. Within five days, Österman noted, his troops had destroyed 80 tanks on the Karelian Isthmus; a pretty good score had the enemy been anything less than the USSR. More had to be done, and General Österman informed Mannerheim's headquarters accordingly. Russian panzers, the kings of the battlefield, had to be stopped. Ditches, mined roadsides, and boulder barricades were not enough. The Finns would have to think of something else.

First, the engineers (Pioneer battalions) came up with the idea of mines made of pieces of steel pipes. The fuse was ignited by touching a trip-wire leading to the pipe, which exploded about three feet above ground. Front-line troops could make these mines by filling the pipes with a mixture they called *klorihartsi*, chloride resin.

Then Colonel Arvo Saloranta invented a wooden-box mine which was nonmagnetic and nearly impossible to detect. The Russians were soon forced to detail their men, armed with spikes, to clear the fields and roads before the tanks entered the area.

But there was more, much more, as Mannerheim's headquarters ordered the formation of special anti-panzer units at every company, battalion, regimental, and division level. The Molotov cocktail was born as the State Liquor Board, *Alkohooliliike*, went to war. Forty-thousand bottles, the regular fifths, were provided, which were filled with the "mixed drink" of crude kerosene, tar, and gasoline. In the early part of the war soldiers wrapped a gasoline-soaked rag around the bottle's neck before igniting and throwing it. Later, ignition was provided by an ampule containing sulphuric acid attached to the mouth of the bottle.

Although the gasoline-filled bottle had been used in previous wars, it was the Finnish Winter War Soldiers who named it the Molotov cocktail. During that time the Finnish army used some 70,000 of them, including 20,000 made at the front lines. It was a horrible fate for the Russian tank crews when the Finns ignited their bottles and threw them, aiming at air intakes or opened hatches. For the Finn guerrillas it meant a casualty rate of 60 to 70 percent. Their only thought was to sell their skins at the highest possible price and to survive as long as they could.

The grim drama of man against tank was seen all along the frozen frontier. It began with the report that the panzers were coming and the anti-panzer men scrambling to their previously dug holes along each side of the road. These holes were carefully camouflaged with branches of

"Hey, neighbor! Death is knocking at your door."
Cartoonist: JUSSI AARNIO. Published by Korven Kaiku. *Used by permission, Oy Lehmus, Tampere, Finland.*

spruce or other evergreens and plenty of snow because the Russian in the turret would be keeping a wary eye for foul play.

Before long General Österman could report that Russian panzers were no longer crashing through unopposed. As anti-panzer units harassed the tanks along the roadsides, other Finnish units doubled in brass to fight the death boxes. Cooks, quartermasters, engineers, and riflemen soon discovered that they could shove a log or a crowbar into the treads of the advancing tank, derailing it so that it was useless. When the tank crews emerged to make their repairs, they were met by Finnish machine gunners.

Panzer crews trying to move across frozen lakes quickly learned that, before the hard frost, their adversaries had set rows of mines just below the water's surface, with pull ropes attached at each end. These watertight mines, partially filled with explosives, had enough air left in them so they hugged the bottom of the ice when the lake became fast frozen. Buoyant metal containers also kept the mines high enough to do the job. The mines were exploded when the tanks were either right above them or just past, so there was no chance for retreat.

The Russians also ran into anti-tank barriers in the ice itself where the Finns had sawed out openings. In areas where they could not keep the "water ditches" open because of the extreme cold, they laid wide strips of cellophane over the snow-covered lakes, hoping to mislead Russian reconnaissance planes into thinking the lake had been opened and that tanks could not cross. They put up make-believe tank fortifications made out of cardboard and even positioned men and horses fashioned from straw so that bombers would waste their ammunition on the fake Finnish "concentrations." There seemed to be no end to the Finns' bag of tricks, but every trick required an individual man of extraordinary courage and even as headquarters officers nodded approvingly at the surprising effectiveness of the crude and unconventional methods of fighting they paid their respects to the lone soldier in the field.

Anti-panzer man Kaarlo Erho could hear the sounds of field artillery as he marched toward the front line and he wondered what it was going to be like up there. He knew that in this sector the Finns were outnumbered ten to one and that a lot of men in his platoon were going to be killed. Who would be the first?

Erho's unit was stationed just behind the front lines; the men had already been assigned to their tents, coffee was on, and everything seemed quite comfortable.

Suddenly a guard called through the tent opening. "Anti-panzer men, get ready with your bottles and ammo. You've got two minutes!"

Erho and his buddy dashed out of the tent to join their anti-panzer group of ten men. Their squad leader, Sergeant Outi Helas, ordered them to dig into the side of the road in five separate positions—men with Molotov cocktails on one side and those with TNT explosives on the other.

Now we are ready, thought Erho. Let them come.

The young Finn had been told that ten Russian tanks had made it through the lines and were approaching his sector. From his hidden position he could see the first lieutenant assigning machine gunners to take care of any tank crews that might try to escape.

The first monster came into view, guns firing in all directions and approaching with such confidence that nothing could seemingly stop it. Eight more of these were following the first, shooting every which way. And Erho thought, "These steel monsters we are supposed to fight with a couple of gasoline bottles and a few hand grenades?" The thought seemed crazy. It would have been wiser to just slowly get up, move back, and leave the whole mad mess behind.

Three tanks had already passed his position and there was still no order to attack. Finally the signal came. Erho released the fuse, counted to three, and threw his bag of dynamite under the third tank. Several loud explosions rocked the ground but when he looked up, this tank as well as the others were turning slowly toward the direction from which they had come. Bitterly disappointed because his tank was not lying helplessly on its side he nudged his buddy, Kivivirta, and indicated he had nothing left to throw.

"Let's get them with this last bottle," the younger man said. With this, he calmly lit the fuse and threw the bottle toward the last tank. It hit just behind the air intake slots and immediately caught fire, reflecting the surrounding area with its yellowish flame. Soon the entire tank was enveloped in fire and Kivivirta said, "Broiled Russians for sure."

In the meantime, Lieutenant Kaarto had tied two three-kilogram TNT bars together and thrown his package into the treads of the second tank, and it was soon motionless on its side. Now the third tank was set on fire by the squad leader himself while the other tanks moved out of reach. The crew of the second tank tried to escape to the woods but this was easily stopped by the men positioned with tommy guns.[1]

[1]Kaarlo Erho, *Summa* (Poorvo, Finland: Werner Söderström, 1940).

6 THE FROZEN HELL OF *TALVISOTA*

At first the Russian soldier did not mind the cold. He had begun his attack on a full stomach and his spirits were high with thoughts of a quick victory. His weapons were big and new, often right from the factory, and the light-weight clothing was only moderately uncomfortable. But things changed as temperatures began to drop to 10, 20, 30, 40 degrees below zero; this was when the real frozen hell of *talvisota*, winter war, began.

In such cold the Red Army soldier's weapons froze, his food froze, his hands and feet froze. If he greased his weapon too heavily, it became useless. If he touched the barrel of his rifle with his bare hand, then pulled it away, he left his own blood. Tank drivers and truckmen discovered that if their engines were not run for a quarter of an hour in every two, their batteries would not work again. Troops needed more food than usual; rations needed to be heavy and hearty rather than hard bread and unsweetened tea if the men were to survive and fight.

In the deep freeze of *talvisota*, human blood froze and plasma was useless. The cold did help the wounded men by stopping the flow of blood, but if they lay too long with torn and bloody flesh exposed, the flesh soon blackened and showed signs of the thin greenish fluid that marks gangrene. Finnish medics stuffed their own mouths with syrettes of morphine to thaw them as they went about their tasks of tending casualties. There seemed to be little of this activity on the Russian side because of the meager, often absent medical aid force. Most of the Red Army soldiers simply froze to death, like grotesque statues, in whatever position they happened to be at the time they were hit.

The Finns also lived with this cold and it was very hard for them, particularly when they made their wide encircling maneuvers at night instead of huddling around a campfire. But few of them had any complaint about the weather; they were accustomed to it and more important the bitter temperatures sometimes saved their lives.

Ensio Nikula tells of an incident at Summa during a severe January day after a heavy Russian artillery bombardment. He suddenly saw a man without headgear or weapon stand up in no-man's-land and begin walking towards the Finnish lines. Since there appeared to be a tattered bit of white camouflage sheet on the man's shoulder, the company commander ordered his men not to shoot, but before the soldier reached the foxholes bursts of Russian bullets had been poured into him.

> We opened his uniform jacket and saw that he was wearing a lamb fur. . . . We counted six bloodless bullet holes in his chest.
>
> Someone said, "Take that man to the tent where the dead are kept. He's gone, for sure. The medics will pick him up in a couple of hours."
>
> The man was left in the warming tent, and about two o'clock that morning when the new shift came back from guard duty, the men lit up their cigarettes and poured hot coffee. Suddenly a voice said, "Hey, give me a cigarette."
>
> We realized it was the "dead" man talking. I lit his cigarette for him and he began smoking, murmuring to himself, ". . . Looks like my legs are okay . . ."
>
> "Yeah, but you've got six holes in your chest," I told him.
>
> "I guess so. I felt a burning sensation just before I got to your foxholes." The man's name was Laaksonen; he'd been stunned by exploding artillery grenades and had been lying on the ground long enough to be half frozen. When he got up to head for his own lines he was hit from behind, with the bullets coming out through his chest.
>
> Laaksonen was quickly taken to the first aid station where the medics explained that the freezing weather had saved the man's life. Normally he would have bled to death.[2]

The Finns were accustomed to the weather, and, more important, were sensibly clothed. They dressed in layers, with heavy underwear, sweater, trousers, and field jacket, and over all this a covering made of bed sheets. The capes and hoods of the ski patrols were described by British observer Sir Walter Citrine as "looking very much like the American Ku Klux Klan."

[2]This account is based on events related in *Miesten Kertomaa*, edited by Ville Repo (Helsinki: Weilin Göös, 1967).

Any of this clothing could be removed, according to the situation. Most Finns were fitted out with a motley array of knitted garments from the home front, lovingly fashioned by little old ladies, housewives, teen-age girls, and anyone who could handle the knitting needle. There were knitted bibs, headwarmers, neckwarmers, gloves, and socks, not necessarily matching but comfortable. These gifts were greatly appreciated. One soldier wrote to a stranger who had sent him a package: "Thank you for the ski suit, and although I don't know what you look like, maybe we could decide on a gesture I could make when we are having our victory parade in Helsinki. Then you will personally know how much I appreciate the gift. It is the best one in Karelia and I won't have to be ashamed to go on patrol in it. As for the kneewarmers, I can be down on one knee, shooting for hours without feeling the cold."

The Russians' light-weight, olive-brown tunics were only slightly warmer than a good dungaree overall. Their underwear was very poor and even lighter than that worn by the Finns in summertime. In the beginning the Red Army was without overcoats.

Unlike the Finns, who had their dugouts and warming tents, the Russians' only shelters were the holes they dug into the snow where they built fires to keep from freezing to death. Their alternative was to cluster around campfires which made them easy targets for the sharpshooters.

Although the Finns had not fought a winter war before, their bodies quickly became so used to the cold that when they did go into a warm tent or dugout, they often complained about the stifling heat. They learned to keep their weapons in action by cleaning them often with a mixture of gasoline and gun oil to prevent freezing. In the absence of antifreeze, they used alcohol and glycerine in the cooling systems of their machine guns.

And so the "moving zoo," as the Finns called their attackers, fought, suffered, and died. By the time they finally faced the main Finnish defense line, their dreams of marching unopposed to Viipuri and Helsinki were shattered. Instead of being met by the happy faces of people they had come to liberate, they found only burning ruins of villages, dark forests, murderous fire from the Finns, and despair within their own forces. The enemy was everywhere; if not on skis, they were behind fir trees, concealed by branches and surprising them with bursts of automatic fire.

For the trained and experienced Red soldiers, the continuous fighting in the bitter cold with meager rations of food and no chance to clean themselves or bathe became a desperate struggle to stay alive. For the raw recruits who knew nothing of army weaponry or discipline, it was disaster. They fought only because there was no turning back; most of them had no real idea why they were in Finland in the first place. They were told that if they were captured, they would be killed. If they turned back to Russia, the *Politruks* would shoot them. Desertion was impossible because even if they escaped the *Politruks*, they would lose their way and freeze to death. If they complained about food, lack of lubricants for their guns, lice, wounds, or frostbite, the *Politruks* carefully noted their disloyal comments in the record books.

Sometimes the men were able to write home, painfully scrawling their messages on spiral notebook paper and sealing them with a piece of wet bread. Thousands of them were found on the bodies of the frozen Russians. "I wonder if there are many people on this side of the front who actually believe that Finland has attacked Russia?" one soldier wrote. "Why were we led to fight this country?"

7 RUSSIAN BOMBS—AND THE BIG SYMPATHY WAR RAGES ABROAD

Russia's plan was to swamp Finnish resistance by simultaneously overrunning the country and cutting Finland in half at its waistline, while aviation demoralized civilians and disorganized the state machinery.

Marshal Mannerheim and his generals recognized the blitzkrieg tactics, copied from the Nazis. There was no subtlety involved; nothing came as a surprise except the wanton way in which the bombs were used. If the home front could hold up under the murderous aerial attacks, maybe Finland's friends abroad would be sufficiently sickened to send help. Perhaps civilian bombings would prove to be the major blunder in this campaign, particularly since the Soviets were using incendiaries.

Communism was supposed to be on the side of the little man, the factory worker, and the modest-income people, yet most of the bombs fell on the sections in villages and cities where such people lived. Their small dwellings were made of wood with sawdust and wood chips used in the walls as insulation against the cold. When bombed with incendiaries, these homes immediately burst into flames and were beyond hope of repair. If these workers had entertained even the smallest thought of the glories of communism, their dreams went up in smoke, along with their houses and worldly goods.

Mannerheim was right in his evaluation of the side effects of such bombings. Not only did they bring worldwide moral protest, offers of help from the West, and eventual expulsion from the League of Nations, but they disillusioned the growing hard-line Socialists and Communists in many countries who had honestly believed in the Soviets' love for the worker and peasant. Simultaneously the bombing of civilian targets blackened the morale of the troops at the front who kept wondering where the mighty Soviet air force was. Why weren't their own planes present to cover them during attacks? Where were the supplies, the food, the bread?

The Soviet troops and the people back home were not told of the civilian bombings. Even into January *Pravda* was reporting that no civilian target had been hit. But with no newspapers from the West coming in with which to compare notes, and no photographs available of the devastated cities, how could the Soviet populace know the difference?

So the senseless bombings continued day after day, and the Finns grew to hate a weather forecast that said, "good weather, clear skies," because that meant the hideous sounds of sirens, the scurrying to shelters where the walls literally shook as explosions rocked the areas above and around them. It always meant the death or injury of someone they knew; in a small country, life can never be impersonal.

There was no real escape from the bombs and strafings of the airplanes, except for the very young children who were bundled up, tagged, and labeled and sent off to Sweden. Many of these children would not return to Finland after the war since they would have no families to come home to. Swedish foster parents would raise them as their own.

The Viipuri-Helsinki train carrying women and children westward was a favorite target for Russian bombing and strafing. When Soviet aircraft appeared overhead, the train stopped and the people ran for the woods or hugged the ground behind protecting rocks. Helsinki to Tampere and all the way to Oulu, the trains were attacked routinely. There was no apparent military advantage in killing civilian passengers, although the disabling of any train or railroad line would possibly cut off the flow of military supplies from Sweden.

Olympic champion Paavo Nurmi, forty-two, was not called into service. His men's clothing store in Helsinki was completely covered over with protective boards. Jean Sibelius, seventy-four and long since retired from public life, reported from his forest home in the suburb of Tuusula, outside Helsinki: "I have two things uppermost in my mind. I am indeed proud of my people and what they are doing these days. And I am happy to witness again the wonderful way in which the great American nation has rallied to the support of Finland."

In the United States there was no doubt about the sentiment towards

Finland, but it was soon evident that words, moral protests, and token gifts would not change the course of the war.

The attack by Russia against Finland had caught Americans by surprise; they were confused as to how best they could help. The first step was a plea from President Franklin D. Roosevelt which he dispatched to Lawrence A. Steinhardt, ambassador in Moscow, and H. F. Arthur Schoenfeld, minister in Helsinki. The identical messages read:

The ruthless bombing from the air of civilians in unfortified centers of population during the course of hostilities which have raged in various quarters of the earth during the past few years which resulted in the maiming and in the death of thousands of defenseless men, women and children has sickened the hearts of every civilized man and woman and has profoundly shocked the conscience of humanity. . . . I am therefore addressing this appeal to the Soviet government [Finnish government in the message sent to Helsinki] as I have to governments which have been engaged in general hostilities, publicly to affirm its determination that its armed forces shall in no event and under no circumstances, undertake the bombardment from the air of civilian populations or of unfortified cities.

This strangely bland message was of little comfort to the Finns huddling in their bomb shelters. It simply told them that President Roosevelt was not taking sides, and that the United States did not approve of bombing civilians anywhere, anytime. America was on record as being against evil.

Joseph P. Kennedy, American ambassador to Great Britain, reported to President Roosevelt that there was no justification for the United States to enter the European war. "If anybody advocates our entering the war, the American public should demand a specific answer to the question: Why." He also said that the American people's "sporting spirit" in "not wanting to see an unfair thing done," might involve us in war, but, he added, "this is not our fight."

More interesting was the step taken by Secretary of State Cordell Hull when he appealed to American airplane manufacturers not to sell planes to a power that would use them to destroy civilians. It had been the practice of Soviet authorities to buy two or three units of the latest and most expensive military planes from the United States. They apparently used these for study and experimental purposes, incorporating the best features in planes of their own production.

Former President Herbert Hoover spoke out strongly on behalf of the Finns, whom he had long admired. He characterized Russia's attack and civilian bombings as a throwback to the "morals and butchery of Genghis Khan," and urged severing diplomatic relations with the Soviets, but the U.S. Congress rejected any such drastic action. Unlike the sudden army of dramatic orators, however, Hoover offered more than just words. He immediately established a fund-raising organization for the relief of the homeless in Finland, similar to the one he had organized for the Belgians during World War I.

In New York City, Mayor Fiorello LaGuardia formed a committee to sponsor a "Let's Help Finland" mass meeting in Madison Square Garden, on December 20, 1939.

The American Red Cross appropriated $25,000 for initial relief measures; an additional $10,000 was immediately sent to London for the purchase of medicines to be flown to the Finnish Red Cross. All Red Cross chapters in the United States were urged to collect contributions for the relief of the Finnish war victims.

Meanwhile American-Finnish clubs and associations formed a relief committee, composed of thirty-nine societies, and set a goal of $1 million to be raised for the Finnish Red Cross.

At the Finnish Workers Educational Alliance, huge cartons packed with old clothes and shoes and labeled with the Red Cross emblem were shipped to war sufferers.

From various parts of the United States and Canada men of Finnish origin headed for New York to go abroad and fight. There were volunteer women, too, who sailed on the Swedish liner *Gripsholm* to do war work and nursing. In Delaware a group of sixty farmers raised $500 for the cause. Four Finnish seamen jumped ship at Portland, Maine, and made their way to New York where they would sail on the *Gripsholm* with the other volunteers. An American pilot signed on, hoping he could organize a Finnish-American flying corps. The oldest of the first group to sail was Jalmari Riukula who had been a chauffeur for a family living in Huntington, Long Island. At fifty-six he was quoted by *The New York Times* as saying, "I am never too old to fight for my country."

Probably at no time in American history had public opinion been so concerned in the fate of a small foreign country. Herbert Hoover, in a speech at Palo Alto, California, was furious that the United States did not withdraw its ambassador from Moscow in protest against Russia's assault on the Finns and the "dead women and children in their streets." He continued:

Why all this tenderness toward Russia? Our government offers its good offices to prevent the attack on Finland. The Administration very properly protested against the bombing of Finnish women and children. We do not even get civil replies. Moreover, has Russia kept her agreement with the United States not to engage within the United States in propaganda to destroy our government?

We should, as was done in Germany, leave a routine official to represent us in Moscow and withdraw the dignity of our ambassador. Mr. Roosevelt gave recognition to the Communist government by treaty and the exchange of ambassadors. That gave them standing as a decent member of the family of nations. We long since have withdrawn our ambassador to the Nazi Government of Germany and we even raised our tariffs 25 percent on German goods. Is the assault on the freedom of Finland and the dead women and children in their streets any less of a shock to us than the Nazi barbarities?

In the U.S. Congress, a request by Finland's Minister H. J. Procope for a loan of $60 million for defense purposes was "being investigated." Even though Finland probably had the best credit in the world, judging from her World War I repayment of debts, there would be no decision made until the end of February, 1940, at which time a loan of $30 million would be granted. This would come too late to help the Finns.[1]

At this time, Cordell Hull made the astonishing comment, "I am against all appropriations since our government would be selling war materials to a warring nation and this would be against international justice."

On December 10 the U.S. Government did give Finland $2.5 million, but the money was to be used for agricultural and civilian aid and foodstuffs. One Congressman said bitterly that "because of these limitations [money could not be used for defense purposes] brave Finland cannot buy anything but powderpuffs and panties. Finland asks for ammunition—we send them beans. When they ask for explosives, we send them tea. When they ask for artillery, we send them broomsticks."

[1]Three years later the United States sent to the Soviet Union: 385,000 trucks; 51,500 jeeps; 14,800 aircraft; 7,000 tanks; and 4 million tons of general supplies.

Two years later, in 1941, Britain and the Commonwealth sent to the USSR: 705 aircraft; 481 tanks; and 2,373 vehicles. Three years later Britain sent the Soviets 1,960 aircraft; 2,795 tanks; and 22,000 vehicles.

The Washington *Post* said, "Finland cannot expect any other help from the U. S. except formal applause."

A *New York Times* editorial stated, "After their work is done in Finland, the Soviets will find among other things, that they have earned the lasting distrust and contempt of the American people."

Dorothy Thompson wrote in the *New York Herald Tribune* of her anger at congressional indecision to allow Finland a loan to buy weapons. She called it "unbelievable frivolity and wantoness . . . the greatest bloodless victory that Stalin has gained so far."

As Congress and the White House debated about whether or not a loan to Finland would set a precedent for all warring nations to ask for help from the United States, Sibelius concerts were being conducted for Finnish relief by Toscanini and Stokowski; American teen-agers were collecting coins on street corners for the cause. Väinö Tanner, Finland's foreign minister spoke out, "We are having a hard time keeping our disappointment to ourselves because the United States could easily help us right now, but they are handling us as though it were a peacetime matter."

And a leading Helsinki newspaper said, "When the building is burning, its owner can't wait patiently for somebody to bring a pail of water. Our borders are burning!"

Meanwhile, Finnish businessmen broke their traditional silence and isolation by volunteering for public relations speeches and fund-raising activities in various parts of the world. For a "salary" of one finnmark a year, they traveled to every conceivable country where aid to Finland might be had. They were particularly vocal in the Scandinavian countries. The mayor of the township of Lauritsala, a Finnish Jew named Santeri Jakobsson, went to Sweden to gain the sympathies of the Jewish population. He did induce the Rabbi Marcus Ehrenpreis to work on Finland's behalf. Businessman August Kuusisto flew to the United States to speak at club meetings and civic organizations.

Such efforts began to pay off. Help came, usually without the official blessings of the country involved. The Finns asked no questions, so long as the volunteers were pledged to their side of the struggle. Eight thousand Swedes signed to help fight the Russians. One Gloster Gladiator squadron, with skull and crossbones markings, was supplied by Sweden and flown by Swedish pilots; in January the Swedes organized a Red Cross hospital in Finland. Eight hundred Norwegians and Danes arrived on the scene and Hungary sent a battalion to fight the Reds. Italian pilots in their

Fiats appeared; a Jamaican Negro and several Japanese showed up. French and British volunteers headed for Finland to help out as best they could.[2] Three hundred and fifty from the United States set sail on the *Gripsholm* but like many well-meaning sympathizers would arrive too late to turn any battle tides.

Meanwhile, newspapers around the world were almost 100 percent on the side of the Finns. The problem here was that the well-intentioned reporters did not have the stories that could have effectively swung help more towards the Finnish camp. Holed up as the newsmen were in the Kamp Hotel in Helsinki, press rooms became an anthill where news was announced—and also created. Foreign correspondents were dissatisfied with the way they were handled, even though the Finnish Foreign Ministry did delegate a news liaison officer who distributed releases from the front. Finns were not famous for their public relations sense.

The Finns took a look at the flood of sympathy flowing their way from around the world and saw that they were only one little cog in the big political wheel. Matters were so confusing that had they not been tragic, they would have been comic. "Neutral" Russia was fighting the Allies in the Black Sea and being fought by British planes in the Baltic. "Neutral" Italy was threatening to intervene if Russia pushed south. The "neutral" Americas, led by the United States, were considering all sorts of measures to assist the first neutral state to be invaded. It was a widening war, and anybody's war; a war so unpredictable that when President Roosevelt announced that American foreign policy was "on a twenty-four-hour

[2]One hundred forty British volunteers arrived about the time the peace was signed. By the end of March, their numbers had swelled to 230, with their leader, Colonel Roosevelt, still in England. Of this pitiful group of idealists, 70 percent were capable men; the others were over-age, some had criminal records, one had a wooden leg, and two had only one eye. In trying to get back to England, 60 of them headed for Oslo at the beginning of April where they landed simultaneously with the Germans. A dozen were taken prisoner and the rest fled to Sweden. Some remaining in Finland tried to make it to Norway through Rovaniemi but the Finns stopped their flights to prevent their capture by the Nazis. Others wound up in civilian life, as loggers, farm workers, or English teachers. One became the pro at the Helsinki golf club. Journalist Harold Evans became a member of the British Embassy in Helsinki. This eventually led him to 10 Downing Street where he served as press secretary to Harold Macmillan. The others traveled with Swedish passports, wound up in German prison camps, or just disappeared.

basis," he was merely expressing the limit of certainty in a world that lived only day by day.

Meanwhile, Mannerheim said of the campaign in general, "I did not think my own men could be so good or that the Russians could be so bad." Then he added gravely, "We have butter but not guns." Because of this fact, he and his generals continued to urge the government to seek peace. President Kyösti Kallio suggested to the Finnish parliament that he would like to write a personal letter to the various government heads around the world, explaining the Finnish position and asking for help in mediation. This idea was rejected as being quite impractical, yet on December 10, parliament did send such a note with the result that materials began coming in from Sweden, France, Great Britain, and the United States. Italy began sending planes and aviators while Britain and the United States sent planes, munitions and gasoline.

In Rome the Pope was "deeply shocked" at Russia's attack; in Budapest students cheered Finland in the streets and shouted anti-Russian slogans. British Prime Minister Neville Chamberlain and French Premier Edouard Daladier spoke publicly against the Soviet drive. In neutral Scandinavia, in Spain, in Japan, public opinion was vigorously anti-Soviet. Even Germany began dispatching rifles and munitions to Finland until Swedish journalists spread the story across their front pages, thus forcing the Germans to stick to the Soviet-German nonaggression treaty. Italy, too, was forced to stop sending materials after the unfortunate Swedish publicity.

During the first week of the war, the United States offered its services as a mediator to solve the problem. The offer was directed to both the Finnish and Russian governments. The Finns immediately accepted; the Soviets coldly refused. Molotov, in a speech on October 31 had said, "It would be better for the United States to concern itself with its own relationships with the Philippines and Cuba rather than get involved with Soviet-Finnish relationships."

The Finns, believing that this was not the Soviet's final answer, turned to Sweden for help as a mediator; at the same time they asked that Sweden look after the interests of any Finns who might still be in Russia. They also informed the Soviets, through the Swedes, that their government was now prepared to make new positive suggestions. Molotov refused Sweden's offer as a mediator, saying that there was no need to discuss matters again because Russia did not recognize any government except that of Otto Kuusinen.

Word finally sifted through to the Finnish minister P. J. Hynninen in Estonia that Russia would negotiate, on the premise that Hanko would be conceded and that Foreign Minister Väinö Tanner would be dismissed. The Finns' reply was that Hanko could not be given up and that the Soviet government had no business telling them who was to be their foreign minister, or for that matter, who any other government official ought to be.

There seemed to be no way of ending the war that nobody wanted. Russia was committed to fighting on Finnish soil and the Finns had vowed they would defend themselves rather than relinquish territory. Other countries nervously sought ways to pacify the adversaries, usually for their own self-interest.

Rickard Sandler, former Swedish foreign minister who had earlier predicted that Russia would not attack Finland, visited Helsinki to talk with Prime Minister Ryti and Foreign Minister Tanner to offer his help as a possible mediator. He urged the Finns not to allow Western powers into Petsamo or Murmansk because this would only mean a continuance of the war and an increased possibility that all of Scandinavia would become a part of the world conflict.

In the "talking war," U. S. Minister Schoenfeld notified Washington that "Finland should be maintained until the 'Political circumstances' changed." The Finns asked Schoenfeld if he would request two neutral countries, the United States and Italy, to bring about peace negotiations with Russia. Schoenfeld promised to do this, but to quote an old Finnish proverb, "The idea fell into the sand . . . without results."

It was obvious at this point that debate, proposals, and long-drawn-out discussions would dominate Finland's "neutral" cheering sections around the world. Emotions ran high and in some cases solutions to the Finns' peril were quite unrealistic. Winston Churchill, after lunching with the director of the Alpine Club, suggested that a group of people who could ski should be collected. "Even a small group of skiers would be almost invaluable," he said.

There seemed to be only one major power remaining silent about the conflict: Germany.

8 | THE AIR WAR

It was at Immola Air Base on the second day of the war that Finnish Air Force Captain Eino Luukkanen arose at 5:30 A.M., climbed into his furs, and walked across the darkened airfield to where the Fokkers were swathed in white camouflage covers. He and his mechanic pulled away the covers of his D-XXI and he climbed into the cockpit. He inspected his machine guns and ammunition belts, then swung the rudder with his feet on the pedals, rocked the stick while watching the ailerons, then signaled the mechanic. The starter whined, the Mercury engine coughed, he caught it with the throttle, and it burst into a comforting deep-throated bass. Luukanen checked his instruments, then chopped the throttle—and waited.

The darkness turned to murky gray and then the sky became a yellowish pink in the east. Suddenly the telephone in the ready room rang shrilly. There were orders to maintain a continuous patrol of two fighters over Vuoksenlaakso. Luukkanen led the second patrol, accompanied by wing man Vic Pyötsiä.

Flying over Enso during the second circuit of the patrol area, Luukkanen spotted two bombers flying towards the northeast at about 3,200 feet. He gave Pyötsiä the signal to attack, then rammed down the throttle, and, with engines roaring, attempted to position himself on the tail of the closest of the two bombers. The enemy, spotting the Finns, banked sharply to the southeast.

The bomber loomed in his sights; 400, 300, 200, 100 yards. With feet planted firmly on the rudder pedals, hands gripping the control column, and eyes glued to the gun sight, he pressed the firing trigger and saw his tracers curve in towards the bomber. Simultaneously, brilliant orange flashes danced in front of his windscreen. It was the dorsal gunner, pumping bullets in his direction. Now his target completely covered his sight and he was forced to break sharply to starboard to avoid collision. Pulling the Fokker around, he again lined up the bomber in his sight, even as the dorsal gunner continued to blaze away.

From his altitude of 500 feet, he suddenly saw several large objects tumbling away from the bomber. The pilot had decided to jettison his load in order to lighten the aircraft and the blast from the bombs tossed his little Fokker around like a piece of straw in a high wind. Once again he positioned himself on the bomber's tail. A little more throttle and he was squarely in sight. He pressed the firing trigger, but as he did so, the pilot of the bomber lowered his undercarriage, which slowed the bomber's speed so that Luukkanen was forced to pull up to avoid ramming it. He loosed a long burst into the starboard engine from about fifty yards; immediately, dirty gray smoke belched back from the cowling. The plane windmilled momentarily, came to a standstill, then nosed down, cleared a clump of trees, and pancaked into a small field.

The Tupolev SB-2, sporting the Red Star, was Luukkanen's first kill of the Winter War and now he could see the crew of three climb out of the aircraft, waving white cloths.

He was very pleased with himself as he landed at his air base and went inside to have breakfast. He was halfway through his first cup of coffee when sirens sounded—an air raid on the field. The low altitude attack by ten SB-2s was all noise and nuisance, however, thanks to the poor aim of the Russian bombardiers. Most of the bombs landed outside the field's perimeter and only one building was slightly damaged. The Finns scrambled to get airborne but only the fourth flight made it, shooting down four of the bombers. The field yielded a Russian prisoner who had misunderstood his pilot's signal to release the bomb load and had bailed out instead. Even at the low altitude, he survived without injury.

A big snowstorm followed this flurry of activity. All aircraft were grounded so Luukkanen used this time to search for the remains of their victims. He particularly wanted to examine their defensive weapons, armor protection, and fuel cells in hopes of ferreting out weaknesses for future reference.At Koljola Luukkanen found his SB-2, a new machine probably straight from the factory but with its fuselage so filled with holes it looked like a colander. He noted that the fuselage was heavily armored but the unprotected fuel tanks in the wings aft of the engine were the Achilles heel of the SB-2. Now he knew where he would aim his bullets in the future.

As for the crew members, the villagers explained that when the Russians were approached the major and two sub-lieutenants drew their side arms. A fight ensued and two of the officers were killed. The third man shot himself in the brain.[1]

If the Soviet tanks, artillery, and masses of men on the ground had been wantonly rammed into Finland's icy forests for their wholesale slaughter, so oddly enough had the crews of 3,000 Russian bomber and fighter planes been dispatched to their own kind of hell. These hastily trained Soviet pilots were no match for their well-seasoned, experienced adversaries; they soon learned that the Finnish fighter pilot was as tenacious a killer in the air as was his counterpart ski-patrol guerrilla on the ground. Although the Russians had their superior "engines in the air," as Stalin called them, to use against the Finns' 162 antiquated aircraft, it was clear from the beginning that the Russians would suffer strangely disproportionate losses.[2] Anti-aircraft fire was alarmingly accurate, but worse were the enemy fighter planes. Soviet bomber squadrons soon developed a strong dislike for the sight of even one lone Finnish fighter plane because they knew that pilot would not let the matter pass unnoticed. Entire squadrons disappeared in their missions over Finland and those waiting for their return to the Estonian base near Tallinn could only guess what happened.

Stalin's "engines in the air" were formidable; their Ilyushin DB-3 bomber was fast and could carry a metric ton of bombs over an 1,864-mile range. They also had their Tupolev SB-2, nicknamed "Katiuska," the first Russian aircraft of indigenous design to be manufactured abroad (in Czechoslovakia). Soviet fighter pilots mainly flew the Polikarpov 1-15 (dubbed "snubnose"), a plane that had seen aerial combat during the early

[1]This account is based on incidents related in *Fighter Over Finland*, by Eino Luukkanen (London: Macdonald and Company, 1963).

[2]"Modern warfare will be a war of engines. Engines on land, engines in the air, engines on water and under water. Under these conditions, the winning side will be the one with the greater number and more powerful engines." Joseph Stalin, November 21, 1939, quoted in: M. I. Kazakov, *Nad kartoi bylykh srazhentii* (Moscow, 1965).

months of the Spanish Civil War and in 1938 on the Manchukuoan border in fighting the Japanese. Occasionally, the obsolete biplane, the two-seater reconnaissance Polikarpov R-5, appeared overhead when the skies were clear.

Their Finnish adversaries had few planes with which to combat this show of force, thanks to the deaf ears on which Marshal Mannerheim's earlier recommendations had fallen. During the eight-year period when the Marshal was chairman of the Defense Council (a period he referred to as "racing the storm"), he made it his duty to study the tactics and military organizations of other countries. Attending military maneuvers on Salisbury Plain in England, for instance, he noted that the French aimed at weight of armor while the British relied on mobility. He later learned that the Germans were extremely interested in the prototype of the so-called independent tank of Vickers Armstrong. (This tank served as a prototype for the Germans' new armor with which their panzers would win sensational victories in Russia, the Libyan Desert, and elsewhere.)

In 1934, Mannerheim revisited England, chiefly to see the air display at Hendon since the re-equipping of the Finnish air force was uppermost in his mind. Later, Hermann Goering invited him to see the newly-forming Luftwaffe in action. The result of these extensive studies was that Mannerheim strongly advocated the use of modern airpower, particularly in the defense structure of a small country. In 1938 he reminded the Finnish government that there were only 200 trained airmen in the air force; at least 600 were needed, and training towards that goal should be started immediately. Modern aircraft should be ordered from abroad without delay. But as usual, his recommendations were put aside while the budget people deliberated the matter.

When the Winter War began, the Finnish air force's newest fighter was the Fokker D-XXI, a single-seater monoplane produced by the Dutch. There were 31 of these, which General J. F. Lundquist, the tall, heavily-built commander of the Finnish air force, formed into the 24th Fighter Squadron stationed at Immola on the Karelian Isthmus. The Finns also had five Brewster B-239 single-seater interceptor and fighter-bombers. These aircraft had been assigned to the U.S. Navy's senior fighter squadron operating from the U.S.S. Saratoga, but in December, 1939, a number of these Brewsters still to be delivered to the U.S. Navy were declared surplus so they could be sent to Finland as a sympathy gesture. The planes were promptly shipped to Trollhättan in Sweden where they were assembled by volunteer mechanics from the Norwegian air force under the supervision of Brewster company representatives. Although the Brewster B-239 had an unfortunate operational career in other services, it was successful in the Finnish air force.

The Bristol Blenheim was the only modern bomber used by the Finns. In 1937 the Finnish government had ordered eighteen of these planes from England and had acquired a license for manufacture of a further twelve Blenheims at the State Aircraft Factory. Dubbed *"Pelti Heikki,"* "Tin Henry," in the Finnish service, the Blenheim operated from Luonnetjärvi near Jyväskylä. Its susceptibility to fire caused the deaths of many bomber crews.

In the air war the Finns had the reverse situation of those on the ground, where the Russians were freezing and the Finns were snug and warm in their dugouts or were at least able to bear the weather because of their clothing and activity. Russian crews flew out of comfortable bases in Estonia or Russia and returned to heated facilities and safety. For the Finns it was night maintenance work by mechanics who labored by flashlight under canvas coverings so they wouldn't be spotted by the enemy. Taking proper care of airplanes flying in such cold weather required the utmost skill and dedication of men who flew in spirit only and who suffered the tight suspense of watching their airplanes take off in pursuit of the enemy. Unless the cylinder-head temperature was correct, there would not be enough power for take-off, and even if the plane did get into the air, the wear and tear on a cold engine could be disastrous to both plane and pilot. Often mechanics worked on their airplanes for two or more hours before morning take-offs, in sub-zero weather. They worked with blow torch, engine cover, and fire extinguisher, blowing hot flames under the canvas coverings so that the heat would penetrate the engine block, allowing all parts of the engine to acquire the normal metal expansion required for efficient operation. The fire extinguisher was always kept at arm's reach; they never knew when the flame would contact grease or gas and set fire to the cover.

In temperatures of 20, 30, and 40 degrees below zero, oil freezes like water, so the Finns usually drained the plane's oil the night before and stored it in a warm place, then poured it in the next morning.

Some of the Fokkers were equipped with skis for use in areas near the front lines where landings were made on the ice. Others had the conventional non-retractable landing gear which made landing in heavy snow a treacherous business.

Seldom did the Finnish pilots have a cozy warm air base to return to; their bases were as mobile as those of the ground forces and were required to be available where needed. An "air base" could mean an abandoned house beside a lake, where they would be camouflaged up to the very moment of take-off, or it could be an elementary school, or hastily erected tent or dug-out, grandly labeled "ready-room." At Värtsilä pilots and crews had no buildings, no telephone communication, and no tents. They stuck a telephone pole into the deep snow and rigged up a field telephone. It was impossible to erect any workable shelters so they passed their alert hours beneath the bare freezing sky, standing in snowdrifts or sitting on the wings of their Fokkers. During their spells of alert duty, they were continually near their aircraft; hot meals were a rarity and they lived on sandwiches and coffee from vacuum flasks.

General Lundquist was well aware of the problems confronting his tiny air force and he was sometimes amused by the stories of newsmen trying to track down his pilots' exploits. One eager writer, learning that Lieutenant Tatu Huhanantti had just shot down three Russian aircraft in one battle alone, managed to get an interview with the pilot. The results could hardly win a prize for reporting.

Question: Would you please tell me how this battle took place? What happened?

Answer? Well, first I shot down one enemy aircraft.

Question: And then?

Answer: And then I shot down another aircraft.

Question: What happened after that?

Answer: I fired again and shot another one down.

Shortly after this interview, Lieutenant Huhanantti was wounded in a dogfight with an overwhelming number of enemy planes. He crashed into a Russian aircraft, taking it with him as he went down in flames. This was his eleventh, and last, kill. His brother Esko, piloting a reconnaissance plane, was also shot down and killed.

Even though the Finnish air force was small, it was writing an unforgettable chapter in aviation history:

Lieutenant Sarvanto: 13 confirmed kills and 4 unconfirmed with his Fokker
Lieutenant Huhanantti: 6 confirmed, 4 unconfirmed
Sergeant Major Pyötsiä: 7½ confirmed, 2 unconfirmed
Sergeant Major Virta: 5 confirmed, 1 unconfirmed
Lieutenant Nieminen: 5 confirmed, 1 unconfirmed
Lieutenant Vuorimaa: 4 confirmed, 2½ unconfirmed

Captain Ehrnrooth (test pilot defending the city of Tampere): 7 confirmed, 4 unconfirmed

And this was only the beginnning of the list.

A world's record was set by the Finnish air force when on January 6, 1940, Lieutenant Sarvanto flew into a formation of seven Russian DBs at 1203 hours. By 1207 the Finn had shot down six of them. All planes crashed and were found. He used 2,000 bullets in this incredible feat. Only two crew members parachuted from the Russian bombers; they were taken prisoner. The rest were killed. Another Finnish pilot shot down the seventh bomber in the squadron.

In the final count of the Winter War, General Lundquist would learn that the Fokkers alone shot down 120 Russian bombers, losing 12 of their own planes in the process, and only 8 men. In all, fighter pilots on the side of Finland shot down 240 Russian aircraft (confirmed). The total Russian aircraft loss, including those brought down by anti-aircraft was 684, and perhaps as many as 1000. The total Finnish losses were 62.

9 THE FIRST MAJOR RUSSIAN OFFENSIVE IN KARELIA: ON-THE-JOB TRAINING FOR THE RED ARMY

> We are doing what every Finnish soldier gladly does against the hordes of barbarians. Yesterday we got about fifty "liberators." They were spreading their funny papers [propaganda leaflets] and we gave them first aid immediately. Ivan has been sowing everywhere around us his so-called bread packages [bombs]. It is a little bit too hard for the Finnish stomach to digest and some of us who happen to get this bread, survive only through an operation.
>
> —*Letter from a Finnish soldier*

The outrageously cheerful Finns continued to harass their enemy even as they dug in at their main defense positions along the Mannerheim Line. The withdrawal phase was over, the Red Army advance had seemingly been stopped, and Christmas was two weeks away. The fighting, what there was of it, soon became strange, erratic, almost stalemated as the field commanders on both sides awaited orders from their superiors. Russian artillery pounded hour after hour, day after day, answered sparingly by the Finns.

The Russians were not sure what to make of the Mannerheim Line, so touted by foreign correspondents and the Finns themselves as being invincible. Soviet commanders immediately added to the legend as an excuse for not breaching the line during their initial thrusts. In reality, this so-called impenetrable area was nothing more than a do-it-yourself line of regular field fortifications, ditches, and trenches. Its main frame consisted of 66 old-fashioned machine-gun nests made of concrete, in front of which were barbed wire, boulder anti-tank barriers (not necessarily continuous), and tree stumps. The line extended for 90 miles; the rest of the 800-mile Russo-Finnish border had no line at all.

The West Karelian Isthmus, which extends from the Vuoksi River to the Finnish Gulf, was manned by the 2d Army Corps (11th, 1st, 5th, and 4th divisions). It was a long frontier, zigzaging through the frozen fields and forests for some 43 miles. The 6th Division in the rear was kept for Marshal Mannerheim to use as a reserve force; no one could call up these forces without specific orders from Mannerheim.

The East Karelian Isthmus was manned by the 3d Army Corps (10th and 8th divisions) on the Taipaleenjoki-Vuoksi-Suvanto line, a distance of 35 miles.

In the center position the Finns had a total of fourteen battalions whose fronts averaged 2.5 miles per battalion. They were scattered mostly on the edges of the woods in a zigzag pattern where machine-gun bases would have the best possible open field of fire. About 250 yards in front of them were anti-tank granite-block lines and barbed-wire barricades.

If ever there were ideal conditions for a Russian frontal attack with heavy equipment, it was here in the open fields of the central Karelian Isthmus. But with the Finns' refusal to come out and fight, thus revealing their weaknesses, the Soviet commanders were faced with the dilemma of trying to break a line they knew little about. There always seemed to be a cannon where there was not supposed to be one, and the enemy appeared out of nowhere in areas reported to be abandoned.

With this kind of frustration, the Reds began sending powerful reconnaissance forces close to their enemy, hoping to get a battle going, but it was no use. Even the strength of the Finns' poorly manned advance battle positions, 2 miles in front of the main defense lines, remained unclear. The pattern of fighting became strangely lethargic. In the morning when the regular "working hours" began, the Russians came, often by trucks, to a point right in front of the advance positions. During these assaults, supported by tanks, the Finns withdrew to their main line. In the afternoon when the "working day" was over, the Russians withdrew some 2.5 miles to their own lines and rested behind their panzers, at which time the Finns returned to their advance positions, often finding materials left there by the Russians.

During these early days of December the Russian Navy continually engaged the Finnish coastal artillery of Koivisto, the Finns' right flank of the Isthmus front. At first they were doing reconnaissance work and clearing the waters of mines in the Gulf of Finland. Then on December 12 the battleship *Oktjabrskaja Revolutsija,* armed with twelve 305-mm. guns and escorted by five destroyers, approached the island fortress of Saarenpää, the island the Russians had earlier asked the Finns to give up during the negotiations. In the heavy fog they opened fire with the heavies from a distance of 15 miles. The Finns returned the fire with a few rounds from their five 254-mm. guns until four of them malfunctioned. That same night the Russian ships continued their action around Saarenpää, with dawn revealing another Russian battleship, the *Marat,* approaching the coast and firing its heavies. Again the Finns returned the fire and after about thirty minutes the *Marat* disappeared, presumably after being hit. Casualties from these actions were slight.

Within a few days of the stalemate's beginning, the situation changed. With fresh Russian troops pouring into the Karelian front, fierce fighting at the main line became almost continuous though the Russians still seemed to have no real desire to penetrate the line. Finns reported hearing explosions and weapon fire far behind the Russian sector, indicating target practice and other on-the-job training exercises. Before long the Finns became convinced that General Meretskov would begin a large-scale attack as soon as his forces were organized. General Österman issued orders to prepare for the worst: rework barbed-wire fences, reinforce machine gun positions, and build more traps and anti-tank ditches. More ammunition would have to be supplied and individual soldiers would have to work around the clock. Rifleman Vesteri Lepistö, a Winter War participant, recalls this period:

Our groups were made up of seven or eight men. The pressure from lack of sleep and rest was so general that the only thought was to get out, do our jobs, and get back as soon as possible. There was always a lack of ammunition; our hand grenades produced in seven different countries were really hazardous. Our lives were at stake every time we used them. Our most aggravating work was getting out there in forty below zero, right in front of the enemy lines to set up barbed-wire barricades. We had to work without gloves and we dared not make any noise. Everything was done at night. . . . I was always hungry. We couldn't eat snow because it was contaminated by grenade explosions and would cause painful stomach problems.

Meanwhile at Summa, even as the 2d Army Corps was preparing for the impending attack on the main line, the Russians suddenly captured one of the Finns' forward positions. The battle was furious and exhausting with the Russian artillery throwing their heavies against the sector where communications man Nikula and Corporal Hakala were trying desperately to repair communication lines. The Red infantry, supported by about 100 tanks, was attacking along the entire front!

Nikula and Hakala ran through the connecting trenches trying to get to their battle positions but the trenches were already occupied by several tanks, one of which was burning fiercely. Three Russians were running away from it but they were soon cut down by Finnish bullets. Hakala yelled at Nikula, "Watch out for that tank!" Directly in front of him a large greasy monster loomed menacingly and Nikula dropped to the bottom of the trench as the tank drove over. The Finn was almost completely buried beneath dirt and snow.

Luckily it was a narrow trench and well enforced so that the walls did not collapse under the tank's 30-ton weight.

The tank stopped above him and continued firing its cannon as frozen sand and gravel, pushed by the panzer's treads, almost completely covered the Finn's head and body; his rifle butt pressing against his chest made breathing nearly impossible. And every time the iron bridge overhead fired its guns, more gravel and snow poured down on Nikula. He finally managed to work his face free so that he could breathe the acrid gasoline-and-oil-filled air, but by then he realized that any moment one of his buddies could very well be preparing to throw a Molotov cocktail. He would be burned alive, along with the enemy above him.

Nikula worked feverishly to free himself but it seemed hopeless. Both feet were immobile and he could only barely move his left arm. The tank continued to thunder.

Suddenly there were different sounds above him; small-arms fire and shouts and then everything was quiet. Nikula was not sure whether he had lost consciousness or whether the Russians had killed every Finn on the front. He sweated in fear and pain and in 30 degrees below zero he knew he would soon freeze to death in his own sweat. He twisted his body and felt his boots come off. Now he was sure his situation was hopeless.

Without warning, the tank moved. More sand, dirt, and snow tumbled down and then the monster was gone. He felt himself being pulled up by his hands and another hand grabbed at his belt. The heavy pressure of the "grave" slipped away but he now found himself unwilling to open his eyes because the tugging hands might belong to Russians. It was only when he heard the dialect of his home district that he knew he was safe. "Hey, Nikula, old buddy. Are you alive or are you dead?"

Nikula opened his eyes. Yes, they were men from his own unit. The tank had left but there were others nearby, immobilized and burning.[1]

Anti-panzer activities would play an important part in holding back the expected enemy drive. The plan called for the destruction of as many panzers as possible, even prior to the main event. Orders from Mannerheim's headquarters stated that any Russian tanks aimed at breaching the line must first be confronted by mines, traps, and ditches. Next would come Finnish artillery fire. The third hurdles were rock barriers and more ditches, and then would come the front line units with their TNT charges, hand grenades, and Molotov cocktails. Behind these units would be the anti-tank cannon. Then would come the regular infantry at the front line and their reserves with their anti-panzer weapons. These reserves were also to place themselves behind the front line to man any tank breakthroughs.

In planning his offensives, General Meretskov counted on the Finns to expect his first large-scale action at the so-called Viipuri Gateway between Lakes Kauk and Muolaa where the country and network of roads would favor large-scale masses of men and equipment. This was his real goal, but he would first slam his forces against the Taipale sector, farther east, in order to draw Finnish reserves away from the western part of the Isthmus. Once Taipale was secured, he would open his offensive on Viipuri.

At Taipale, close to the frontier, the lake makes a bend towards the south, around a spit of land forming a good bridgehead, with the Finns' line running right across the northern part of the promontory. Here at the eastern end of the Mannerheim Line foxholes and trenches were little more than drainage ditches built by farmers to keep swamp water from flooding their fields. In many places the trenches were so narrow it was almost impossible for one man to pass another. It was at Taipale, between December 6 and 11, that the Finns engaged in some of the most remarkable defensive actions of the Winter War.

[1] This account is based on events related in *Miesten Kertomaa*, edited by Ville Repo (Helsinki: Weilin Göös, 1967).

Niilo Kenjakka, platoon leader in the 21st Division, arrived with his men to relieve the linemen who had been in position for the past several days:

In telling my men what positions to be in I gave them an order: "This is your spot, kid, and over there is the enemy and you are not to let him in here." I couldn't help but think about the long complicated orders that we learned in military training and how quickly the realities taught us to be simple and straightforward in our orders. My boys didn't ask any questions, they simply took their positions . . . some on one knee, some just standing against the bank of the ditch and with almost childish obedience began to look into the darkness towards the enemy. Older men, as they were leaving, whispered advice to the younger boys: "Be ready for the baptism of fire because the enemy knows you're green and will try his damndest to break through so you'd better hold these positions. Otherwise they'll have to call on us to come back and counterattack.[2]

As anticipated by Mannerheim, the Russians stormed across the ice and open country in masses, stubbornly refusing to change any of their tactics, in spite of weather, terrain, and murderous crossfire. The attacking division's losses were so brutal that it had to be withdrawn and a fresh division put in. The latter attacked on December 15 but was thrown back, losing 18 out of 50 tanks. The following day, after eight hours' artillery barrage and four hours' continuous bombing, the Russians penetrated the Finns' positions in two places, but by nightfall the Russians were thrown out and the Finns' lines were again intact. The following day the Finns surprised the Russians with a heavy artillery attack which broke their offensive spirit and forced their withdrawal. On December 17 the enemy threw in a third division, with no more success than before.

Meanwhile, as the fierce battles of Taipale raged, Mannerheim was watching the massing of enemy troops in the direction of the Viipuri Gateway. There was greatly increased air reconnaissance along with numerous attacks in which the Russians suffered heavy losses of tanks. (Within a two-week period 108 tanks were destroyed in the West Isthmus alone.)

On the morning of December 17 an intensive artillery barrage opened up between Summa village and the railroad. At 10:00 A.M. the first attack was launched against the Finns' position east of Summa and on Summa village itself, a little *point d'appui* on the highway to Viipuri. As usual the

[2]Ibid.

enemy drive was preceded by a five-hour-long heavy artillery barrage, supported by some 200 aircraft and numerous tanks.

The Finns had expected to be fighting two divisions and three panzer brigades at five different sectors. Now it was discovered that the Russians were using four additional infantry divisions and two panzer brigades (120,000 men) to attack the two sectors of Summa and Lake Muolaa. In the heavy fighting the Russians were able to make a slight penetration at the cost of 25 tanks, but by evening the whole line was again in Finnish hands.

Events clearly indicated lack of creative leadership within the Red command; they fought according to the rule books and there seemed to be no deviation even when the situation called for it. The Russian regiments were grouped one behind the other; panzer units were given orders as to what day they were to participate. When one regiment and panzer brigade had completed their program, they withdrew to rest and lick their wounds. The next in line took over where the other left off, having been unsuccessful in breaking through. When each regiment and panzer brigade had done their job, the assault was over for them.

The tank crews were perhaps the bravest as 30-ton panzers in clusters of 20 to 50 fearlessly approached the Finns' main defenses with their tight formations of foot soldiers following close behind. They found themselves crashing into rock barriers and tumbling into ditches, fighting rocks with explosives, and sometimes firing directly at the obstacles. By December 19 some 50 tanks had burst through the Finn lines all the way to Summa village, hoping to carve out pockets in the rear, only to find their own infantry retreating. Many of the panzers were destroyed and the rest slowly clanked back to their own lines, leaving behind at least 50 percent of their comrades.

The fighting continued from morning till night on December 20 when all attacks were finally beaten off before nightfall. The five-day battle was over, the Russian troops had withdrawn out of sight, and the Finnish 5th Division could happily report that the main defense system was intact with no breakthroughs left open. Behind and in front of the Finns' lines lay fifty-eight destroyed tanks, twenty-two of which were the heavy ones. Thousands of frozen bodies lay quietly in the snow, sometimes in heaps, sometimes in long rows like toppled dominoes. Grotesque statues, bits and pieces of humans were soon covered by a fresh snowfall as Finnish soldiers gathered up the rifles, grenades, and ammunition of the fallen Russians. They found letters and diaries which they turned over to headquarters;

it was soon clear that the Red soldiers, in spite of their massive numbers and superior weaponry, had serious troubles of their own:

We march already two days without food prepared in the mobile field kitchens. In this severe cold we have many sick and wounded. Our commanders must have difficulty in justifying our being here and finding our way in this strange territory. . . . We are black like chimney sweeps from dirt, and completely tired out. The soldiers are again full of lice. Health is bad. Many soldiers have pneumonia. They promise that the combat will end on Stalin's birthday, the 21st of December, but who will believe it?

When news of the defeat in Karelia reached Leningrad military headquarters, surprise was almost unanimous. Few of the top leaders cared to remember Artillery Marshal Voronov's earlier warnings of possible difficulties in Finland. And even Voronov had been mistaken about the value of the Finns' Suomi submachine gun.

In Voronov's words: "Only after the actual invasion did we recall that way back in the beginning of the 1930s we had acquired a model of the Suomi submachine gun, which was even tested by a commission of specialists on infantry weapons. The commission decided that it was a police weapon, unsuitable for military combat operations. Now, having encountered the widespread use of submachine guns in the Finnish army, we bitterly regretted these miscalculations."

Even more than guns, the Russian military leaders regretted they had underestimated the individual Finnish soldier. Vice Admiral I. I. Azarov spoke out in retrospect: "The determination of the Finnish soldiers and their fighting skill, we considered an anomaly. To speak openly of such phenomena was considered reprehensible. Scorn for the enemy did not allow the commanding personnel and the political workers, particularly those who had not taken part in the war, to reconsider the concept which had become rooted in our circles—that victory would be easy—and to prepare themselves and their troops for a war more difficult and severe than military games, drills, and maneuvers led them to expect."

Nikita Khrushchev reported in his memoirs; "Stalin was furious with the military, and with Voroshilov—justifiably in my opinion.[3] Once Stalin jumped up in a rage and started to berate Voroshilov. Voroshilov was also boiling mad. He leaped up, turned red and hurled Stalin's accusations back into his face: 'You have yourself to blame for all this! You're the one

[3]Marshal Klementi E. Voroshilov, people's commissar of defense.

who had our best generals killed!' Stalin rebuffed him, and Voroshilov picked up a platter with a roast suckling pig on it and smashed it on the table."[4]

In spite of angry recriminations, regrets, and temper outbursts, the fact remained that the war had to terminate in a Russian victory before spring, and the breakthrough would have to come at the most important front, the Karelian Isthmus.

If for no other reason than to save the prestige of the Soviet Union, a new southeastern front was ordered to be formed with additional and well-trained troops. Marshal Semyon Kostantinovich Timoshenko, a former barrel maker who had served in the czarist army as an NCO when Mannerheim was a general, would be given the responsibility of breaking the Finnish defense lines at the Isthmus. Timoshenko had the advantage of youth, for he was still in his early forties, and was in favor with Stalin. He had recently returned from Poland, where he had taken part in the Soviet occupation. An imposing figure with shaved head, gray eyes, bass voice and stern features, Timoshenko agreed to undertake his assignment only after being promised that he would not be held responsible for any great Russian losses in the process. Timoshenko was a very practical man.

[4]Nikita Khrushchev, *Khrushchev Remembers*, (Boston: Little, Brown and Company, 1970), p. 154.

10 | THE KARELIA DEFENDERS COUNTERATTACK

The Russians' first major offensive in Karelia to occupy the Viipuri Gateway had ended in their clear defeat. The Finns in the principal theater had stood up to greatly superior forces far better than Mannerheim had hoped, and, although artillery continued to sound and minor fights kept both forces active, a relative lull settled over the front. Many Finnish soldiers hurriedly wrote letters home:

Not much is happening here. It's everyday stuff. Airplanes are flying at treetop level, firing their machine guns, but we are deep down in our dugouts. Some of the men are shooting, some are sleeping, some are going to sauna, some are fixing coffee and there is always a lot of humor. The trees around our dugout are being broken off by the Russian artillery but we don't pay much attention to that. We are short of ammunition and we have figured that it doesn't really pay to fire until you see the enemy's beard shaking.

The men at the forward observation posts were kept busy. One of these soldiers wrote to his family:

Some time ago the Russians were playing their loud speaker and we enjoyed the music very much. However, we were looking forward to hearing the propaganda speeches. We have it figured that every time Kuusinen starts talking, the Russians stop shooting so we won't miss a word of the speech. With the Russian guns quiet, we can make a break for the "head." All of us readily admit that the enemy's propaganda is a very convenient thing.

In the odd patchwork of the December fighting in Karelia, both the Russians and the Finns experimented with weaponry. The Finns dragged into position a pre-World War I Russian field cannon that someone had discovered in the village park. On careful examination they found that although the firing mechanism was of World War I vintage, the weapon was mounted on a stationary platform and there was no recoil mechanism. No one knew what would happen when they rammed the artillery shot into the rear of the cannon, locked it, and pulled the rope hanging from the back, but the challenge was too intriguing to resist.

The explosion was deafening as the cannon jumped nine feet backwards, leaving a big cloud of smoke hanging in the air. Within a few minutes, the men got the gun back in the same position to repeat the process, but this time they assigned two observers: one to see where the shell landed and the other to see where the cannon went. The Finns enjoyed their *Hyppy Heikki*, Jumping Henry, even more when they learned that at least one large-sized Russian truck had been blown to bits.

Everyone in the Finnish battalion was now eager to see the relic, but by this time the Russians were taking the thing seriously. Every time the cannon went into action, enemy mortars opened fire in an attempt to quiet it. At one point they fired on it for three hours without interruption. In time, the crew of *Hyppy Heikki* became quite clever; they would fire four or five rounds, then leave the cannon and go to their tent for coffee. After several days of this activity, Russian mortars got their first hit on *Hyppy Heikki*. One of the spokes on its wooden wheels broke, a spoke that cost the Russians 10,000 rounds of mortar.

While *Hyppy Heikki* kept the Finns amused, the Russians occupied themselves with developing some new weaponry behind their own lines. Finns who were snooping around or in forward positions could hear sawing, pounding, and excited conversations as the "carpenter/sheet metal factory" prepared the new secret weapon—the panzer sled. On the wooden sled was perched a steel box which would accommodate twenty men. A tank would push the sled filled with troops.

Also prepared in this "factory" were steel shields designed to protect advancing infantry soldiers. In the center of the medieval shield was a hole through which the rifle protruded.

The Finns were bursting with curiosity, and one day Corporal Vermu, after seeing the shields through his binoculars, said, "Hey, let's go get some of those. We may need them ourselves."

Vermu received permission from his platoon commander, rounded up six men, and the "sheet metal platoon" skied down through no-man's-land towards the Russian lines. They returned within the hour without their shields. Corporal Vermu said there would be some coming in a day or so.

They did indeed come in a trial assault, but were soon thrown away in disgust and the Finns could have as many as they wanted for souvenirs. The panzer sleds proved to be equally useless; bullets could penetrate the metal boxes.

It was clear to Marshal Mannerheim and to Lieutenant General Harald Öhquist, commander of the Finnish 2d Army Corps, that morale and humor among these troops were high. Conversely, prisoners of war had reported that enemy troops were exhausted, many were refusing to advance, and a number of death sentences had been carried out. Also, it could be assumed that for a time, the enemy would be short of ammunition and fuel. The enemy's temporary weakness invited measures to anticipate a counteroffensive; active intervention, moreover, would further stimulate the fighting spirit of the Finns who hated their static defense role.

As early as December 11 General Österman, Finnish Commander at the Karelian Isthumus, had proposed a counteroffensive, but Mannerheim turned him down; the Finns were too split up and knowledge of the enemy's groupings was too incomplete at this point. Also, the Finns could not be thrown against the strong Russian armor without effective anti-tank arms. "No," said Mannerheim, "it is far better to await the attack in entrenched positions." Nevertheless, even as the battle of Summa was raging, the Marshal had given Österman the authority to use the 6th Division for a counterattack, in the event of deep penetration of the line.

This division, reinforced by an infantry regiment from the coast defense, was to participate in a counteroffensive in which parts of five divisions were to attack between Kuolemajärvi and Muolaanjärvi. The objective was to break up heavy Red concentrations in these areas; if the attack was successful, the offensive could be widened all along the front.

Österman's plan depended on the surprise element, therefore there could be no large troop movements behind the lines that might be spotted from the air. Also, there could be no artillery preparation.

It was an extremely daring plan because it called for removing men from their defense line positions for the first major assault. The problem was that every advancing unit was tied to its defense section in a more-or-less straddling position—defending the line while at the same time attacking.

The zero hour was fixed at 6:30 A.M. on December 23.

The Finns' troubles began immediately as heavy Soviet air bombardments blasted them. In their confusion they realized that a number of key personnel they had come to depend on had been transferred elsewhere. Worse was the fact they had earlier lost contact with their adversaries so they had little idea of where the concentrations were now located. Too little time had been allowed for preparation and without modern radio equipment the whole operation was soon doomed. Exhaustion after the long night's march was another problem. One Finnish company commander from Group S later explained what happened:

We arrived two hours late at our assault positions and the cause seemed to be a comedy of errors. Men who had left their main defense positions for the initial assault had worked feverishly to open their own barbed-wire defense lines, and to make roads for our troops to march through their own minefields. But when the battalion was led to the spot where there was supposed to be an opening in the barbed wire, they couldn't find it. A little further to the east, they did find an opening, but it was just a routine one used for a single patrol as an exit. So it took the battalion an hour and a half to get through. The weather was clear, about eighteen degrees below zero, and soft snow was up to the men's knees. Skis which had been received the previous day were still in their factory packages; the bindings in one place, the skis in another. So we didn't bother with them. This was probably a good decision.

Communications for the Finns were miserable or nonexistent. Telephone lines lying across the road or on the ground were continuously broken by troops marching over them. One battalion, coming from behind, decided that the feeble lines belonged to the Russians so they gladly and faithfully broke them. The Finns finally resorted to the use of runners and messengers for communications.

Requests for artillery, mortar fire, and anti-panzer cannon seemed to fall on deaf ears or on the wrong ones. The Group S company commander continues his lament:

When we reached an open field about two and a half miles from our assault positions it was already 12:30 P.M. In front were ten Russian tanks pouring murderous fire over our heads and there were many Russian soldiers dug in on the opposite side of the river. It would be hopeless to try to break through without artillery. A request was made to the only battery having direct communication with the company; the surprising reply was, "We can't shoot over there. It is out of range." "What battery is this?" It suddenly became clear that our own Group S and Group Vuori artillery support batteries had switched signals in the early dawn confusion so we weren't even talking to our own artillery batteries!

Single battalions had no idea what was going on in the neighboring sectors, even though they could hear the sounds of fighting on both sides. From the southeast, in the direction of the main railroad, sounds indicated that somebody was retreating. As one Finn soldier put it, "We were wondering if the toes of the boots had already turned homeward. We figured that this human spearhead might not suffice against panzers. Somebody reported that our neighboring battalion had not been successful in its assault."

After two nights of marching and fighting, the toll began to be felt; without roads field kitchens did not reach the front lines, and the men, particularly those wearing rubber boots, were suffering from frostbite. Evacuation of the wounded was a slow, painful journey with sled and skis. Morale and attitude of all the men plummeted badly.

The Finns' big attack advanced some three quarters of a mile to about 2.5 miles. Some moved easily, some with difficulty, but by that afternoon of December 23, they had been stopped all along the line. General Öhquist, commander of the 2d Army corps, gave orders to halt the offensive and withdraw back to the main battle positions.

Though the offensive had not achieved the desired results, the unexpected Finnish activity did have an effect on the enemy. It would be six weeks before the Russians would make any significant moves against the Mannerheim Line; meanwhile the Finns would concentrate on wearing down the enemy piecemeal. A soldier's letter describes life on the front in those weeks:

It is forty-seven degrees below zero on the Molotov front and the Russians are dancing around the camp fires to keep warm. The Finnish artillery put a big *kapsakki* [the Finns called their shells a "suitcase"] right in the middle of it. The Russians are nervous because they've been stuck in the same area for nearly a month. The other night they had their loudspeaker on and said if the Finns didn't surrender within forty-eight hours they'd bring in the Germans and kill us all. Well, forty-eight hours later we are still here, and we figure our bullets will kill Germans as well as Russians.

Still smarting from their heavy loss of tanks, the Russians stepped up their air activities, began using more artillery, and stopped the bunched-together mass attacks by the infantry. Instead, the infantry resorted to what the Finns called "groundhog tactics." Small squads would crawl along ditches into bushes and into holes made by grenades. They dug in the snow by pushing metal panzer sheets in front of their skis, hoping to establish small, weak positions within the Finnish barricades where they could act as listening posts and reconnaissance units. The small attacks the Red soldiers made from these positions were quite ineffective.

The biggest such "groundhog" nest was made on December 20 near Muolaa Lake, following the first Russian offensive; the Finns called it the "Oinola boil." An entire battalion of Russian soldiers, with their artillery and tanks, lived there all during the stationary war phase. A number of "pimples" (companies) were also dug in, but they were eventually destroyed.

Odd weaponry continued to appear on the Karelian front. One Finnish soldier wrote: "The Russians have a new weapon. Our boys call it the Russian coffee grinder because it looks as though they pour buckets of bullets into a machine gun and grind out the shots. Their aim is very bad and only a few times was anybody wounded."

Another invention was a mine "rake," a contraption attached to the front of the tank. This was supposed to explode the deadly nonmagnetic wooden-box mines without causing damage to the panzer. Operationally, the tanks were quite safe, but the metal spike "rake" was seldom effective.

There was also the so-called self-operating machine gun. This would automatically open fire when an object passed in front of its barrel. It was probably a welcome invention for men who were fearful of the dark; the robot allowed them to catch a nap in their trenches. The obvious difficulty was that the rays could only point directly ahead, and the Finns could easily avoid *that* situation.

The Russians began using observation balloons which greatly improved the accuracy of their artillery fire. The balloons were in the air night and day, tethered 1.5 to 2 miles from the Mannerheim Line. At 1500 feet their view of Finnish activities was excellent, and the Finns were now obliged to use darkness as a cover for movements of reserves and supplies.

Also during this period, the Soviet air force began actively bombing front-line soldiers. It was not uncommon for a single aircraft to follow one or two Finnish soldiers on an open field and empty its ammunition supply on this small game. A Finnish soldier wrote:

One day I was standing guard on the bridge when a Russian plane tried to bomb the bridge. Bombs fell on both sides; one fell only two meters from where I was hugging the ground, and the other landed five meters on the other side. I was covered with a lot of gravel and my face was dirty, but the bridge was still there.

The Russians, even though they had stopped the Finnish offensive, were not jubilant over their success. They seemed to be going nowhere and each day they became more depressed. A Russian soldier wrote:

Dear brother-in-law. Now that you have also been called to fight for a fat well-being, I personally would give up my economy, everything I own, if I didn't have to fight this war. The offerings have been plentiful; more on our side. We have been sending tanks, artillery and infantry against the Finns with no results . . . just killed comrades. Sometimes as many as 300 after our attacks, and the Finns won't let us pick them up. Their fire is extremely accurate and they mow us down as with a sickle. A couple of days ago we sent 147 men to attack and only 23 returned. So far, nothing great has been achieved for our cause. The fight against the Finns is extremely difficult. We have not been able to push them back from their defense lines and we can see much suffering ahead of us. We should encircle them since our bombs don't seem to do the job. The Finns are hanging on to their ground.

Meanwhile, the Finns, sadly digging in after their ignominious repulse, learned that the Russians had only recently fired ten rounds of artillery on the city of Viipuri and as a result many of its remaining civilians had fled to the country. Rumor had it that the cannon fire came from somewhere near Perkjärvi, 6 miles southeast of Summa, and gossip somehow tied it all to the Finns' unsuccessful attack. On Christmas Eve the rumor circulating around Viipuri had Russian panzer and motorized columns approaching the city. General Öhquist dispelled these fears with the news that the ice in front of Viipuri would not as yet hold such heavy equipment. But the continued long-distance "ghost" artillery kept everyone in a state of suspense. The situation was further aggravated by reports that a secret Finnish code had disappeared from one of the division headquarters and a new one would have to be created in haste. This meant a period of complete radio silence which added to the fears of many.

Rumors continued to fly. On December 24 coastal guards near Viipuri spotted a small truck column, just about the only such vehicles the Finns owned. But they were mistaken for Russian and the alarm was increased. Russian panzers were "seen," but on further investigation it was learned that the "panzers" were actually seven rock formations protruding through the ice. Such rumors had a strong effect on the morale of soldiers and people in the rear who could not know what was happening, so that many soldiers begged to be assigned to the front.

The Russians did not always fight in masses. Some individual soldiers acted as spies, the *desantti*, who were dropped by parachute behind Finnish lines and on the home front. Wearing Finnish uniforms and carrying small radios, their task was to send information back to their own side. This activity amounted to very little, since most of the *desantti* were killed on landing. *Lottas* and older men on "sky watches" reported them even as they descended beneath their parachutes and a reception committee was invariably waiting for them. Some were met by Finnish peasants armed with pitchforks; others simply turned themselves in as prisoners of war.

The Russians seemed to have no interest in camouflage. In darkness the Finns could see the large camp fires; during the day tracks in the snow revealed the number, directions, and locations of the main Russian troops further back. Artillery batteries were usually set up in open fields without any camouflage; the snow in front of the cannon was black and revealed the burned debris of firings. Finnish aircraft could easily spot tank tracks. They often bombed Soviet planes that were sitting out in the open with no coverings to hide them.

The Finns characteristically were as secretive as possible. Artillery was located in forests rather than on the fringes. Treetops were replanted on the roofs of fortifications, over trenches and dugouts so they could not be spotted from the air. Horses were "dug in" to protect them from shrapnel and only a few were left close to the battery itself. From the air, roads in the forests were like a labyrinth going nowhere. If the Finn had to be outside his blacked-out tent or dugout, he preferred to be in the darkness rather than risk a campfire.

The Mannerheim Line continued to hold; as the days went by, everyone seemed to agree that this was a vital morale factor. Often the Finns fought bloody battles just to regain a little territory that was not even strategically important. Communications problems were constantly with them. Because light artillery batteries did not have radios, the entire communications traffic was forced to go through a single heavy artillery radio station. When they received orders for fire from the observers there was no time for questions because their hands were already filled with orders for the light batteries. But in spite of the unorthodox system, the Finns performed some amazing feats with their artillery.

An artillery officer describes the feeling:

Suddenly the only connection behind my position was broken because of enemy action and now all fire requests were for my battery. The attack had already advanced to a point where the light batteries were only firing to prevent infantry advancement (heavy artillery could no longer participate). I received a message that there was a breakthrough at M [target] number 5197. "Fire!"

I could not give this order to the light batteries because concentrated barrage was not needed. The enemy had just taken a forward Finnish machine-gun base and was now firing at the breaking point. The battery commander and I decided to concentrate our fire in front of the line, using the cannon that had had the best accuracy up to that point. We fired two rounds of our most sensitive shells and two minutes later I heard somebody say, "Hey, you did a good job. The enemy is fleeing." I sighed with relief because with 150-mm. shells you cannot afford to concentrate the fire. The nearest shell had fallen only about 120 yards in front of the Finns.

What actually happened in that battle at "M number 5197" was that three tanks, after having penetrated the anti-panzer boulders, had gotten as far as the Finnish trenches. A fourth one was moving alongside the trenches blasting with a flame thrower. Two companies of Russian infantry were following them through the broken barbed-wire line. At this point the Finnish artillery opened fire. The first shells landed right in the midst of the two companies, causing enormous casualties. The Finns had never seen such panic because now, the second salvo landed in the middle of where the Russians were heading. The shaken Finns screamed with relief and happiness. Two of the tanks were destroyed, along with the flame thrower.

Now came a radio message that there were forty panzers advancing toward the line and they were clearly visible to the artillery communications officer. This time they were advancing on a wide front—like a parade. It was a beautiful, overwhelming sight. Finnish artillery accurately hit to the right of the panzers, surprising the entire column. They immediately scattered in various directions and some turned back. A few were immobilized; one in panic drove straight toward a swamp, got stuck, and sank.

Guns and artillery were not the only noises on the Karelian Isthmus. Propaganda leaflets and words over the loud speakers were as thick as snowflakes in a heavy storm. *Politruks* passed out reading material to the Red soldiers: "We are fighting for the land of our birth, for the workers and peasants' government, and for Stalin. We are helping the Finnish national government to achieve freedom and independence. Soldiers, Red officers and all members of the Red Army, do not under any circumstances give yourselves up as war prisoners. Forward in the name of Lenin and Stalin."

Finnish propaganda at the front consisted mostly of leaflets distributed by patrols and airplanes. The main theme was based on the right of Finland to defend herself against Russia, and a comparison between Finnish democracy and the Russian system. Later on the Finns began to emphasize the terror and horror of war and induce homesickness in the Russians: "These are your choices; refusal to go into battle and go home —or give yourselves up as prisoners—or white death . . . frozen in the forests of Finland." To emphasize their points, the Finns began attaching pictures of skulls on tree branches and focusing lights on them.

The main goal of the Finns at the Karelian Isthmus was to keep their defense line intact and to carry on whatever corrosive, nerve-racking harassment they could manage until some kind of rescue or relief arrived.

The Russians busied themselves with return harassments and forceful reconnaissance in the hopes of softening the Finns' line prior to the big breakthrough which their leaders told them was imminent.

If the secondary purpose was to exhaust the Finnish defenders, the Russians had succeeded. The Finns were dead tired. For weeks they had been on the alert almost twenty-four hours a day, even when they were not actually in battle. Heavy artillery and Soviet aircraft had made movement behind the lines almost impossible during daylight hours; all such activity had to be done at night. Replacements, transporting of the wounded and dead, reinforcement of the dugouts, repairs, inspection tours, patrol activities, regrouping of troops—all were done in darkness. Mail deliveries, newspapers, orders, parcels, and situation reports reached dugouts almost regularly at four A.M. And because Russian artillery and mortar fire sometimes continued throughout the night, nobody had much sleep. Guard duty was extremely exhausting and even the hardy sportsmen such as champion skier Pekka Niemi, who was a patrol leader, were ready to collapse with fatigue.

Because of the chaotic day-and-night schedules there was continuous light in the dugouts. In front of the regimental and battalion headquarters, men read newspapers at four in the morning. Some commanders worked on their plans for tomorrow's activities at two in the afternoon while they were having their morning tea. Men went to breakfast at eleven o'clock at night.

And sometimes the Finns on the Karelian Isthmus sang the song, "I came home yesterday today, and I'm coming today tomorrow."

Meanwhile, north of Ladoga all the way to Petsamo there were no defense lines or trenches and the Finns were in their own element. Operating on a company or at most a battalion level, with quick, flexible movements around and behind the enemy lines, they literally forced the attacking enemy to fight defensive battles. The Finnish soldiers, one of whom was Olympic gold medalist in speed skating, Birger Vasenius, were tough, athletic, champion skiers, accustomed to their terrain and climate.[1] Also the majority of these men were reservists, defending their own homes and villages.

It was in the north that the Red Army found its nemesis.

[1]Birger Vasenius was killed while leading a ski patrol northeast of Ladoga. Champion skier Pekka Niemi survived the war.

11 | IN THE NORTHERN WILDERNESS

The fact that winter in the northern latitudes was more advanced [than at the Karelian Isthmus] was an advantage to us. We had to beat the advancing columns before they had emerged from the frontier districts to more populous parts, where the road network offered better communications and would make it possible to advance towards the railway Sortavala-Nurmes-Oulu.

In this situation, I had to make some of the weightiest and most important decisions of the Winter War. Everything pointed to our main position of the Isthmus soon becoming the object of a general attack . . . but the enemy's unexpectedly rapid advance on this front had compelled me to alter my plans. Instead, I directed a large part of my meager reserves eastward to Tolvajärvi, Kuhmo and Suomussalmi."[1]

Northern Finland has a stark, rugged beauty all its own. Rooted in time, the landscape's serenity and spaciousness can be traced back to millions of years of glacial erosion when sharp peaks were made smooth and rough places made plain. With the coming of the Ice Age, 10,000 years ago, the country was covered by a sheet of ice, beneath which low hills and valleys were formed. As the ice melted, the land rose above the waters and thousands of lakes and islands along the coast and inland were born. The country became a land of forest, water, and rock, giving it a mysterious, primeval timelessness which even the hand of man could not noticeably change.

[1]Carl Gustav Mannerheim, *The Memoirs of Marshal Mannerheim* (London: Cassell & Co. Ltd., 1953), p. 332.

Forests of pine, spruce and birch cover nearly three-fourths of the land, thus giving rise to the proverb, "Finland without forest would be like a bear without fur." Green gold is the term used to describe the forests, because of their importance to the country's economy. In central and northern Finland the graceful birch trees are overpowered by the more study evergreens, but in the farthest north all trees dwindle in size and number as the arctic tundra takes over. Some Finns have said that if Finland had been blessed with Norway's mountains, the Russians would never have dared invade her. But the Finns' land is generally horizontal, rarely rising above 600 feet. Their highest point is Lapland, where reindeer roam over the scenic fells and the nomadic people care for their herds with no regard to boundary lines.

In such areas people could never have survived all the hardships of history and climate without that quality known as *sisu*, which loosely translated means "guts." The country gave the northern Finn a stolid, rocklike obstinacy, patient endurance, and dogged courage, closely akin to the ancient formations on which he lived. *Sisu*, combined with violence which is the counterpart of the loving-kindness of the Finn, had always made him a dangerous adversary in war. Now, as the Russians moved in to take over his country, the Finn identified with the land so strongly that he would die rather than lose it.

The Finns of the north had been on skis from the time they were small children. They had lived with and loved their wild country all of their lives; few had traveled more than a few miles from their birthplaces. As youngsters they had played the game called *suunnistaminen*, or orientation in the forest. School children were given a compass and a list of checkpoints within the woods where they were to make contact at a stated time. Hidden behind trees, instructors made sure the young Finns reached their designated checkpoints. These northerners were experts at finding their way in the vast wilderness; their war tactics were based on the simple question, "Why go into an open field and get shot at when you can have the protection of the forest?"

The twenty Russian divisions attacking the north in their usual tight spearhead fashion were not enchanted by the beautiful frozen lakes and heavy forests. Many of them had marched almost 200 miles in eleven days, from the Murmansk Railway, and had lost much of their strength to frostbite. Seldom did the troops have a roof over their heads and evenings were spent looking for dry wood to make a campfire. They would collapse beside the fire, with one side of the body burning, the other side freezing. When they crossed into Finland, even this luxury ended.

Operationally, these divisions hoped to combine all their forces that were advancing from various directions, once they reached their designated goals, and from then on proceed westward through Finland's inland road system. Once these forces were joined, all resistance would be crushed.

The plan was plausible until they crossed the border and ran into problems not covered in their war tactics. Snow drifts three to seven feet deep forced them to detail twenty- to thirty-man platoons to tramp the snow into hard surfaces so that equipment could pass. Worse still was the swampland beneath the snow that had not yet completely frozen. During the late afternoon a soldier could sink a foot into the slush and be completely soaked; at night the freeze would set in. For heavy vehicles the Reds devised a "tramping detail" of thirty men on skis, followed by 200 infantry men with heavy boots. Much of the time they simply shoveled it out of the way; a slow, creeping, inglorious process that aggravated the condition of the already exhausted officers and men.

The columns along the northern invasion routes extended for 18 to 25 miles, beginning with the division reconnaissance units (advance guards), then the forward units (advance guard reserves), followed by the forward troops (one regiment with field artillery), a panzer battalion of some fifty tanks and supporting units, then the main force of two regiments and the main field artillery units. These long snakelike columns were supposed to have their flanks protected on both sides by patrols marching along on parallel roads about two or three miles away. Obviously Soviet intelligence had not been consulted; roads in these sectors were 30 to 40 miles apart and the only security possible was in areas a few hundred yards from the main column.

At the border the advancing spearheads met only weak forces of border patrols and companies who simply stalled and harassed them. They found no anti-panzer fortifications like those of the Mannerheim Line in Karelia and no anti-panzer weapons threatened their slow-moving columns. They should have been jubilant but they were not. All around them, the silent forests beckoned with *bielaja smjert*, white death, and no one dared leave the road and protective artillery for fear of disappearing forever. These troops without skis were completely inexperienced to life in the woodlands and wilderness; without compasses or orientation, foot soldiers had no idea where they were in this strange dark land.

The eerie silence was short-lived. Before long, the roads to which the Russians had clung for safety became frozen graveyards as Finnish patrols, fighting singly or in small groups, began surprising their camp sites with deadly strikes. Skiing swiftly out of nowhere, wearing white hoods and capes, they slashed at the sides of the spearheads in full confidence that their adversaries could only release small forces at a time for actual battle. The guerrillas also knew that the panzer force, artillery, and air power were useless in the woods.

Even those divisions lucky enough to find Finnish dwellings still intact often met with disaster when they tried to use them as headquarters. Ski patroller Toivo Marttinen described what happened at the village of Aittojoki.

In the predawn darkness he, along with his group, stood on his skis, hung onto his poles, and waited as Lieutenant Perälä slowly skied past the line of men and stopped in front of Marttinen. Frost formed on the lieutenant's bearded face; leather belts held his hand gun and map sack across his chest. He whispered into Marttinen's ear, "So this is your home village. You know the area . . . the enemy is headquartered in the house furthest to the left."

Marttinen nodded. "That is my home."

Perälä continued, "We will slowly sneak up to that house and destroy as many of the enemy as we can. We have orders to burn it along with the other houses. But headquarters is most important. You and I will go first." Marttinen's story continues:

I bent over my skis to make sure my bindings were tight, removed the safety from my submachine gun, and placed it across my chest. Then we quickly skied toward the house, past my sauna where I had taken numerous baths. The snow around the building was undisturbed and through the window I saw a piece of candle and a book of matches; there was a faint smell of charcoal and rotting birch whisks.

We stopped and inspected the buildings from a distance. Everything was quiet except for the sound of horses' hooves in the barn. The lieutenant grabbed my arm and pointed out the guard standing in the shadow of the entrance to the house. He was armed with an automatic rifle, and in the courtyard were several stands of stacked rifles, which meant there was probably at least a company of Russians in the main building.

I gave my submachine gun to the lieutenant, dug out my handgun, and

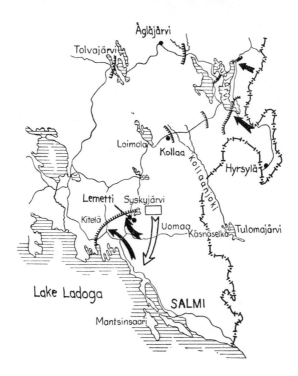

The basic Finnish defense plan North of Lake Ladoga was to stop the enemy at Kitela-Syskylake Line. At the same time the Russians were to be halted at Susjärvi area by multiple defense positions, if necessary.

released my skis. The guard began moving toward us and I froze. He didn't see us so we started crawling on our bellies through the snow, just as I'd done as a kid playing war games. I felt the sweat of fear on my back and tried not to breathe because I was right behind the guard.

I slowly eased myself into a standing position, my arm reached around his neck from behind, and I hit him on the head with my gun. Then we quickly dragged him to a place between the house and the barn.

The lieutenant signaled to the others to surround the building; hand grenades and Molotov cocktails were distributed . . . I sneaked onto the porch where strange smells met me, but the squeaks were the way I remembered. We could hear men snoring inside as we threw two or three hand grenades and some Molotov cocktails into the kitchen. They exploded before we could leave the porch and we could see the explosions from all the windows. There were loud voices, and people trying to get out of the building only to be met with murderous fire.

I headed back to my skis and the woods as bullets flew over our heads . . . I saw a cord of word I'd cut earlier that fall and remembered eating my lunch at one of those woodpiles. . . . I skied, thinking of my childhood—hardly noticing the line of blood I was following . . . the wounded being dragged in the *pulkkas* [sleds].[2]

Because of the unsuccessful attempts to break the Mannerheim Line at the Isthmus, the Russians decided to step up their pressure on the unfortified area immediately north of Ladoga. The plan was to advance the 168th Division, commanded by General Bondarev, from the Salmi area toward Koirinoja-Kitelä and join the 18th Division, headed by General Kondrasev, which was moving on the Uomaa road toward the Lemetti road crossing. In this operation the Russians had been successful. However, as early as December 9, Russian LVI Army Corps headquarters realized that other divisions marching toward Kollaa were far behind and could not join the 168th and 18th as planned. With the 139th and 75th divisions already in the Tolvajärvi area, the 18th Division turned north toward Sysky Lake, some four miles north of Lemetti, with orders to secure the northern flanks of the 168th Division and to attack the Finns defending Kollaa at their rear.

It was at this point that Mannerheim realized that his calculations concerning the forces the Russians were concentrating between Lake Ladoga and Lapland were far too optimistic. He had assumed that supply difficulties would discourage the enemy from using more than three divisions in this northern front. Now it seemed that because the Russians had, in 1939, vastly improved the network of their roads toward the Finnish border and had continued the construction of the Petrograd railroad toward Suojärvi, large supply stores had accumulated near the Finnish border. Therefore, in the early phases of the war, the enemy surprised the Finns by putting seven divisions into the sector immediately north of Lake Ladoga, increasing the number to ten in the course of the conflict.

Mannerheim was now faced with perhaps the most crucial decisions of the Winter War. Knowing that ultimately the main Soviet drive would be at the Karelian Isthmus, he nevertheless parted with his meager reserves and deployed them to the north. Adding strength to the 4th Army Corps by creating Group Talvela, his orders were that when the Russians reached the Tolvajärvi-Ilomantsi area, they were not only to be stopped or pushed back, they were to be destroyed.

[2]This account is based on events in *Miesten Kertomaa*, edited by Ville Repo (Helsinki: Weilin Göös, 1967).

Leading this critical campaign was Colonel Paavo Talvela, who had written his War College thesis on theoretical battles that might occur in the Tolvajärvi sector. This tall, slim farmer's son was a realist, with strong, almost stubborn personal opinions. Now he would see what would happen when his small forces challenged the Russian 139th and 75th divisions with their manpower strength of more than 45,000, their 335 artillery pieces, 90 tanks, 50 panzers, and heavy mortars.

Serving under Talvela was Lt. Colonel Aaro Pajari, the energetic, blond, broad-shouldered former commander of Tampere's Home Guard. An independent thinker, he would become known for always being in the front lines with his troops.

Talvela arrived in the sector with the 16th Reservist Infantry Regiment along with various logistic units, and on December 10 a few anti-panzer platoons appeared on the scene. By Mid-December, some 9,100 Finns were in the Tolvajärvi area with their twenty pieces of artillery.

Talvela's troops were older reservists and although most of them came from the cities, they were accustomed to the terrain of the wilderness and could handle themselves well in difficult situations. The Russians, particularly those of General Beljajev's 139th Division, were for the most part poorly trained White Russians; some 60 percent had received no military training at all and only 30 percent had served in the Red Army before coming to Finland.

When Colonel Talvela had first reached the front, he found the Finns in complete chaos. They had been withdrawing almost continuously during the nerve-shaking days since the war began; many of them were in a state of near panic. On December 7 Colonel Pajari found the 7th Bicycle Battalion fleeing in confusion before the Russian panzers after completely abandoning Kuikkajärvi Narrows which they had been given strict orders to hold.[3] They were quite literally all over the woods, miles from where they were supposed to be, and it took some time to round them up. Some were later found wandering around as far away as 18 miles after having lost most of their weapons and other materials.

The enemy had captured the area around Matkailumaja and Kotisaari and was now in the position to threaten the village of Tolvajärvi itself. In desperation, Pajari rushed the newly arrived 3d Battalion from 16th Infantry Regiment to defend the Tolvajärvi-Hirvasjärvi line and the following day reinforced them with the 9th and 2d battalions and one artillery

[3]Bicycles were used during summer operations; skis were used in winter.

battery. The situation was extremely grave. At nearby Ilomantsi things were equally bad.

Something would have to be done immediately if the rapidly advancing enemy were to be halted. Some balance had to be achieved, some time gained from a short defensive battle, after which the Finns could regroup for a counterattack.

Colonels Talvela, Pajari, and Stewen reviewed the situation and finally came up with a plan which they hoped would wrest the initiative from the enemy and break their momentum. With the two antagonists mixed higgledy-piggledy over the entire area, no one knew for certain who was in what village or on what lake. Under these conditions even routine defense seemed questionable, if not impossible. The Finns would begin their plan with two simultaneous assaults which if successful would gain for them the time needed to create their own initiative.

On the night of December 8 Colonel Pajari sent a company and a half to encircle the enemy near Taivallampi and hit the Russian battalion at their campsite. At the same time Captain Ericsson with his 7th Bicycle Battalion, which was by now reassembled and back in order, attacked the Russians at Kotisaari. Captain Ericsson was killed in this battle, and his battalion skied back after completing a reasonably successful assault. Colonel Pajari's night strike was a complete success. The Russians were so confused in the darkness that two of their battalions fought each other for two hours.

But these small accomplishments only temporarily disturbed the Russian 139th, now impatient to move forward. On December 10 the division began an over-all frontal assault. One Russian battalion soon encircled Hirvasjärvi and was in position to hit the rear of Talvela's group from the north. Pajari, who was enroute from division headquarters, discovered the Finn's predicament and immediately decided to counterattack with a hastily assembled force of 100 artillerymen and troops from headquarters. At the same time he ordered the 1st and 4th companies of the 16th Regiment, which had been held in reserve, to strike from the east towards the road on which the Russians were advancing. The Finns later called this bizarre battle the "Sausage War" because the Russians, after their long march through the wilderness, were hungry and exhausted. After capturing the Finnish field kitchen with its hot sausage soup bubbling on the stove, the troops began eating instead of fighting. Many of them died with Finnish sausage in their mouths.

Further south the Russian 364th Infantry Regiment with one battalion swarmed over the ice at Tolvajärvi to slash at the 9th Company of the 16th Infantry. Snow clouds hung over the frozen lake; visibility was bad, and in the fierce fighting 180 Russians were killed. As the Finns collected Russian weaponry and mortars, they found that 110 of their own had been wounded and 10 killed, including their commander, First Lieutenant Purasmaa.

There were other battles that same day with heavy casualties on both sides, but by now the Finns could see that the aggressive Russian battalions were scattering themselves over wide areas. Their positions were not as secure as they had been only a short time before. The Finns determined to disperse them even more.

Colonel Pajari decided on a daring, surprise assault aimed at gaining the upper hand, the initiative so badly needed. On December 12 Pajari and his troops shouldered their way across the icy fields to capture Kotisaari. Finally, all Finnish units reached their prearranged blocking line at Kotisaari and Kangasvaara. The fighting was desperate; Russian losses were terrible. Among their dead was the commander of the 609th Infantry. The entire regiment's documents were captured, and the Finns were surprised to learn that the Russians had not known of the arrival of the Finnish 16th Infantry. The Reds thought they had been fighting only four battalions of Finns.

The Russian division had clearly been beaten during the day, a large part of their weaponry confiscated, and some 1,000 Red Army soldiers counted dead. The Finn advance continued on the next day. Near Ristinsalmi the Russian defenses held for a while, but the following day even those positions were taken.

Now the Finns were facing fresh troops from the 75th Division. The exhausted pursuers with their heavy casualties finally stopped their advance, but Mannerheim's headquarters demanded that the drive be continued.

The following day the three Finnish battalions resumed their eastward push and finally captured the trenches of the fleeing troops of the 75th Division. At Ala-tolvajärvi the Russians had dug in and the Finns faced strong opposition. As soon as these lines were taken, the pursuers continued to the east where 2 miles beyond they found another strong line of Russian defenses. It was later learned that these lines included recently arrived graduates of the Red Army Officers School in Leningrad and the battles were the bloodiest yet faced by the Finns. There were attacks, counterattacks, and finally one Russian battalion succeeded in pushing through behind the Finnish unit. Lieutenant Martti Siukosaari, company commander, received orders from Colonel Pajari to keep up the pressure and not allow the enemy to dig in. Siukosaari was forced to use everything and everybody he could round up, including artillerymen, quartermasters, and engineers, to destroy the Russian battalion.

By December 17, while still inflicting heavy casualties to the withdrawing enemy, the Finns reached the peninsula between Särkijärvi and Ägläjärvi. Here, the enemy was well dug in and a heavy snowfall made everything difficult, even for the Finns. Their skis sank into the deep snow and maneuvering was very tiring. Heavy bombardments by Russian aircraft kept Yläjärvi, Tolvajärvi, and Haukivaara booming with explosions. The confusion was so intense that the Russians accidentally bombed their own troops.

Colonel Pajari knew his men were tired, but he stuck to his basic tactic of keeping on the move in order to save bloodshed. He would allow one day of rest for himself and his troops; they would regroup their units for the attack on Ägläjärvi village that same evening, December 21. By 1530 hours the following day the Finns had captured the village.

The next day the Russians were pushed to the east bank of the Aitto River near Suojärvi, where they would remain in their trenches for the duration of the war.

Now the weary Finnish troops and their officers could have at least a brief rest. It would be unwise to chase the Russians any further to the east, particularly since they were already reinforced with fresh troops. The Finns in their exhausted condition could not sensibly challenge them.

Colonel Talvela could now report to Marshal Mannerheim that between December 12 and 23 a few Finnish battalions had pushed back 36,000 Russians, along with their panzers and what was left of 335 cannon, some 25 miles towards their own borders. The Finns had lost 630 killed and 1,300 wounded and although the enemy had not been completely destroyed, their casualties were extremely heavy. The Russians lost over 4,000 killed and 600 became prisoners of war. The Finns confiscated 59 tanks, 3 armored cars, 31 artillery pieces, 220 machine guns, 142 light machine guns, and more than 3,000 rifles. They found 150 light automatic weapons along with motorized vehicles, trucks, and horses. The lighter weaponry was distributed immediately to Finnish units on all fronts while the heavier equipment was sent to repair factories. Much of it would find its way to the Karelian Isthmus.

The victory at Tolvajärvi had far-reaching effects. Had the 139th Division pushed through unopposed, the results would have been disastrous to the entire Finnish defense effort in Karelia. Talvela's skill in forcing the 75th Division into the wilderness, where the Russians fought at a disadvantage, prevented it from participating in battles further south.

For the Finns on all fronts, and at home, the victory was a badly needed morale booster. The people were given new heart in the uneven struggle; now they could see that their sacrifices were not in vain.

From the Russian point of view, the defeat of the 139th and 75th divisions at Tolvajärvi, along with the news of what was happening to the 163d and 44th divisions at Suomussalmi and Raate Road, greatly affected the two Russian divisions at Petsamo. No longer would the well-trained 104th and the less elite 52d drive further into Finland; the risk of the 104th sharing the same fate as the others was too great. They would dig in and set up their defenses. The Petsamo area, too, from now on would be considered stabilized.

12 | INSIDE THE PINCER CLAWS

The village of Suomussalmi had a population of 4,000 or less before the Russians arrived. These Finns were mainly blue-eyed, blond Tavasts who made their living as woodsmen, farmers, hunters, and fishermen. There was no wealth or heavy industry; even the roads were poor. The countryside was the most beautiful imaginable, with magnificent tall, snow-cloaked pine trees that glistened in the sun. By December 7 the village had been evacuated, its Home Guard and reservist defenders withdrawn behind Lake Niskanselkä and the entire area put to the torch. There would be no supplies or shelters left for Major General Selendsov's 163d Division advancing from Juntusranta in the north, and there would be nothing for the Russian 44th Division advancing along the Raate Road from the south. Not that the 44th needed anything from the Finns; they were in fact supposed to have delivered supplies to the 163d as early as December 3. But the two divisions were a long way apart and the Finns had orders to keep them so.

Selendsov's plan was to destroy the Finnish troops at Suomussalmi village against the backdrop of the frozen ice of Haukiperä and Niskanselkä lakes. The defenders were to be pushed onto the lakes by the pressure of the 44th Division advancing from the southeast. On the unprotected ice, they could easily be annihilated. The 163d was not to occupy Suomussalmi village itself because the two long narrow lakes on either side of the peninsula could prove to be a death trap.

The Finns knew this and had deliberately withdrawn to more advantageous defense positions. As matters turned out, the 163d, in its exuberance at having advanced so successfully to the burned village, could not resist the temptation to take it over, even though it offered no supplies or shelter. Surely they could hold out until the 44th division joined them.

The two Russian divisions were extremely powerful. Their combined manpower was 48,000 and they were bringing with them into the Suomussalmi-Raate Road area some 335 cannon, more than 100 tanks, and 50 armored cars. The Finnish defenders, now reinforced, totaled 17,000 men; they would eventually have 11 cannon.

The troops of the 163d were mostly Mongols, poorly trained but considered capable of doing a job. The 44th Division, however, were crack Ukrainian troops from the Moscow Military District. Led by General A. E. Vinogradov, this parade division with its band instruments and smart uniforms was slated to lead the victory parade in Oulu, 150 miles to the west.

The officer that Marshal Mannerheim sent to the Suomussalmi-Raate scene was Colonel Hjalmar Siilasvuo, a tough, shrewd officer who was a thoroughly qualified military expert. His entire manner was individualistic, daring, and stubborn. Serving as chief of staff was the capable Captain Alpo K. Marttinen, of the regular army. Mannerheim also released to Siilasvuo the 27th Infantry from his own 9th Division reserves.

Siilasvuo's immediate task, on arrival, was to set up headquarters in the house of the district forester at Hyrynsalmi village to study the situation and plan his strategy. First, the Finns' position must be strengthened, and since artillery was not yet available, machine guns and mortars would have to suffice. He knew the battles were not going well for his forces and that the Russians were continuously building up their strength with fresh troops. If the 163d and 44th ever joined, it would be all over for the defenders. Orders were to deal with one division at a time.

Of great concern was the unprotected northern flanks in the snow-covered woodlands. Colonel A. V. Viklund, representing General Tuompo's headquarters, devised a plan for using military police for such duties as securing and reconnaissance. These well-trained, well-equipped light units would not be hampered by the regular infantry's heavy equipment. They could dispense with the old rules of limiting encircling maneuvers to 3 miles and, instead, ski as far from the main front as 20 or 30 miles. The three-to-five-hour ski journey would be a tremendous athletic feat, particularly when they would then have to engage in heavy fighting, but the surprise element would be worth the effort. The use of the military police was an ingenious solution to an otherwise insoluble problem.

Even as Colonel Siilasvuo struggled with the battles against the 163d, he was constantly aware of the slow-moving 44th Division on the Raate Road. The road must be cut immediately; the most obvious spot was at the mile-wide isthmus between Lakes Kuivasjärvi and Kuomasjärvi, about 6.5 miles from Raate village. He knew that the forests had helped the defenders in other areas, but at this particular isthmus, Finland's frozen lakes would offer a strategic advantage to Lieutenant Colonel J. A. Mäkiniemi's two companies from the 27th Infantry, which he sent to block this key area. Any movement by the Russians on the ice of the lake would be detected by even a lone machine gunner and could result in mass slaughter. The only alternative for the Ukrainians from the plains would be to go into the dense timber, leaving behind their heavy equipment and this they would be unwilling to do. It would be a good plan if it worked, but could 350 Finns close the isthmus against an entire division?

After a number of bloody hand-to-hand surprise battles, Siilasvuo's plan did work and the isthmus was closed. Finnish military writer Colonel Y. A. Järvinen later explained the action against the 44th at this point. "Usually before an operation, the patient receives an anesthetic so that he will not suffer unduly during the surgery, or kick too much. So before the operation began [in which the Finns were fighting the 163d] small local anesthetics were applied [to the 44th], the purpose of which was not to alleviate suffering but to prevent the patient from kicking. In order to numb the long, huge Russian snake, numerous small encircling operations were applied alongside its body." The paralyzed 44th Division was stopped, in bumper-to-bumper traffic, and there it stayed—locked in the Finnish pincers until such time as Siilasvuo's forces undertook the "final surgery."

Meanwhile, 6 miles north at Suomussalmi village, troops of the 163d desperately tried to push the Finns further west by attacking across the frozen lakes. The Finns were under constant pressure, exhausted, cold, and without hot food. Clothes and footwear got wet and both Russian and Finnish troops agonized in pain with frostbite. There was hand-to-hand fighting with side arms, bayonets, hand grenades, and knives; a campfire was an impossible luxury. Both forces were without food supplies; the Russians because of the non-appearance of the 44th, and the Finns because their mobility prevented any quartermaster units from following them. Everyone fought, including the "brass."

As a sample of the fighting, consider an encounter near Suomussalmi village. The forests thinned out there and the open terrain offered little protection for the Finns. Two tanks appeared, their guns blazing. The Finns immediately took cover behind stumps and trees. Lieutenant Huovinen, Captain Sihvonen's adjutant, managed to tape together five grenades, then began crawling with them towards the tanks. First Lieutenant Virkki followed Huovinen and when he had come within 35 yards of the tanks, he stood up and emptied his pistol into their observation slots. He hit the ground as the tanks began firing their machine guns.

His comrades were certain that Virkki had been hit, but after a few moments, they saw him struggle to his feet and fire his pistol again. The tanks' machine guns sprayed the area a second time as Virkki again flattened himself on the ground. The scene was repeated again and now the tanks turned to head back towards the village.

Meanwhile, Lieutenant Huovinen had crawled up close to the tanks from behind, but was not in position to throw his grenades. As the tanks turned in retreat, he ran after them but whenever he got close enough to toss his grenades, they increased their speed. Finally, he gave up the chase, but the enlisted men watching the scene were inspired by their officers' fearless actions. Shortly after this battle, another first lieutenant, Remes, after having been wounded in the hand, headed for the first aid station. His body was found the following day—amidst six dead Russian soldiers.

The Russians finally gave up their unsuccessful attempts to push the Finns further west and simply withdrew to the village to await the 44th's arrival. On December 11 the Finns now felt sufficiently confident to begin their counteroffensive, which lasted continuously for seventeen days. They attacked Suomussalmi and all along the road to Juntusranta, 50 miles away, closing the claws of the pincer and destroying the segments of the enemy columns. At long last the Finns saw the Russians, one by one, leaving their positions. Soon there were hundreds of them gathering on the ice at Kiantajärvi near the Hulkoniemi peninsula. They formed columns, preparing to withdraw across the ice toward the northeast on the 22-mile-long lake. Weapons had all been thrown away, and now the columns became longer and longer as the defeated men moved slowly through the deep snow covering the ice. Along the roadsides, in temporary shelters, in dugouts, everywhere were the bodies of Russians who had been frozen solid like badly executed waxworks. Papers, pamphlets, vodka, atlases, school copybooks, even music scores were scattered everywhere.

Overhead, Russian bomber and fighter planes circled aimlessly, sometimes shooting at a wooded area in the hopes of hitting Finns who might try to prevent the strange exodus. Finnish Colonel Mäkiniemi sent two machine gun platoons along the east side of the lake to "help" a few of them along the way. Another light Finnish guerrilla company, which had been operating on both sides of spider-like Kiantajärvi, soon received word to be prepared to meet and welcome the marchers. A week later Finns found individual Russians still wandering around lost in the surrounding timberlands.

One such soldier was discovered among several dead comrades beside a machine gun base. He had been hit on the helmet by Finnish bullets and had lain there for three days. On interrogation he explained that he was a fish packer from Archangel. "I was visiting [Russian] Kemi on business and I even bought my wife a pair of shoes. They're still in my pack. I was about to leave town when I came face to face with the commissar who took me by the coat lapels and asked why such a healthy young man as I was still running loose when the army needed every man in Finland."

The Finns gave the man cigarettes and a pair of socks because he had none. Then they took him to their dugout and kept him as a mascot for several days, feeding him, giving him drinks, taking him to sauna, and watching him dance *ripaska-pikku ryssää.* (Russian peasant dance). He was finally turned over to the P.O.W. camp.

For all intents and purposes, the 163d Division could be considered to have been eliminated as a fighting force. It had suffered a terrible and humiliating defeat, leaving some 5,000 dead on the battlefield as the remnants scattered into the frozen wilderness in the off chance that they might make it back to Mother Russia. The 44th Division was supposed to have saved them but didn't even try. Their planned assault on December 28 could possibly have saved both divisions but, as the Finns later learned, the orders were mysteriously canceled. As long as the Suomussalmi battles were raging, the 44th had a chance of victory, but after that, even if they had broken through Kuivasjärvi Isthmus, it would have meant no more than changing the scene of their destruction.

Once the Suomussalmi battles were over, the Finnish main force skied south over the ice of the lakes to begin chopping up the 44th Division's traffic jam on the Raate Road. Since they had earlier opened the roads towards the main direction of their attack, the Finns could easily transport their recently acquired booty from the Suomussalmi battles; trucks, horses, cannon, field kitchens, and just about anything they felt would be

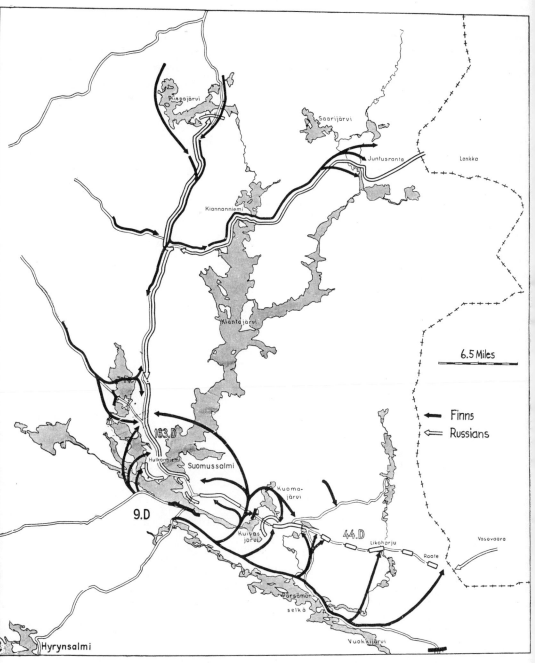

The Finn operations against the Russian 163rd and 44th Divisions at Suomussalmi and Raate Road during the war *Courtesy: Werner Söderström Oy, Helsinki, Finland*

useful. By reassigning the Suomussalmi victors immediately, Colonel Siilasvuo was counting heavily on the excitement of the recent success to carry the troops through, in spite of their fatigue. The officers and men now had an unshakable faith in their ability, and they were all convinced that a new victory could be won if they would go after it. Technically, Siilasvuo figured that his forces would now be in the position to attack from the north as well as the south—simultaneously.

The main forces of the Russian 44th Division were located on the road between Kuivasjärvi and Kokkojärvi, a distance of 5 miles. They had "secured" the road with platoons about one-eighth of a mile apart, all 15 miles back to the Russian border. Between these platoons, tanks patrolled endlessly back and forth.

One of the first Finnish actions on reaching the road was to build strong anti-tank barriers of fallen trees and barbed wire. Their recently acquired anti-panzer cannon would take care of any tanks that made it through these barricades.

Now, they attacked the head of the long Russian column with the strength of two battalions, about 800 men, and the results were as Siilasvuo had anticipated. The enemy began to fortify, dig in, turn passive, and cancel all offensive plans. This gave the Finns time to regroup their Suomussalmi forces for the final blow against the 44th.

On January 1 four Finnish companies attacked the heavily manned and fortified Russian battalion near Haukila. The following day they repeated the assault, this time with the strength of two battalions, and after heavy fighting advanced to the east and south side of Haukila village. The Finns on the east side cut the road and immediately built field fortifications around the road's breaking point. By holding these positions regardless of heavy Russian counterattacks, the Finns had cut off the head of the giant snake.

But snakes live a long time, even without their heads. Nevertheless the Finns were convinced that the Russians, regardless of their powerful material force, could not successfully attack during the time that was needed for the final "surgery." They had deliberately planted the notion that their forces were far more powerful than they actually were. The 44th Division assumed that only great numbers of their enemy could simultaneously engage both the 163d and themselves. The Finns hoped this image would continue to pacify the 44th.

Siilasvuo carefully shifted his forces. The fighting was almost always hand to hand, and in this type of warfare the Finns excelled. In the darkness friend and foe were often identified by the peaked Russian headgear or the ability to sing the first line of the national anthem in Finnish. Heavy artillery was useless; units that were pulled by horses trying to escape added to the traffic congestion and to the mounting chaos. The Ukrainians had no help from their tanks, particularly after the roads were cut and mined. The Finns, who had been using tree stumps as fortifications, now began to realize that destroyed tanks provided excellent cover. They were horrified to see those panzers that were able to escape driving over their own material; even the infantry was pushed against the road blocks and quartermaster vehicles.

No military officer could untangle such a mess; orders could not even be heard. Soviet airplanes circling around could only helplessly watch the miserable situation below. Any bombing or low-level attacks could easily kill their own troops: 17,000 Russians in a five-mile area, going every which way, provided a spectacle to the Soviet pilots that none could believe, even as they saw it happening. Perhaps Soviet aircraft could have destroyed some of the Finns' supply lines, but even that would have come too late. The Finns had purposely scattered their details over a wide area and had carefully camouflaged them. Besides, any occasional destruction of Finnish supplies would be more than adequately compensated for by the spoils they had just taken.

Three small Russian reconnaissance planes did try to drop food to the troops of the 44th, who by now were almost mad with hunger and the cold. Each plane carried two bags of hardtack, that is, six bags of food for the entire division.

Russian officers repeatedly asked General Vinogradov to order a retreat; the troops were in no condition to fight anymore. But the general refused, saying he would have to have orders from "higher up." Finally, by January 6, with the Finns' constant pressure, Vinogradov announced by radio to all regimental headquarters that the retreat would begin not earlier than 9:30 that night. But the orders came too late.

The men no longer had the strength or spirit to break through; they panicked and ran, or were shot down in shelters and dugouts without an attempt to escape. It was later learned that the Soviet troops had been without food for five days in temperatures of 30 to 40 degrees below zero.

Although most of the men of the 44th were killed or frozen, 1300 of them became prisoners of war. An officer found in the woods told the Finns about how his commanding officer had been severely wounded so he took over the command. "But the regiment was almost completely decimated. Then I was wounded, and helped by an NCO and two of the men. By ten P.M. one of them was shot; an hour later another was killed, and by one A.M. I was alone." The officer had dragged himself through the forest for four hours in the direction of the Russian frontier.

He was found by a Finnish ski patrol at nine that morning, collapsed in the snow and half frozen. His captors gave him a hot drink and two men carried him on their backs for nearly two miles until they could get to a stretcher. He was given first aid in a forest hut, taken on a sledge to a field hospital, and finally to the P.O.W. camp.

A nurse first class attached to the 44th Division told how she had been called up on September 7. She was married and had a two-year-old baby, but because she was not a nursing mother, she was recruited along with two other nurses; they crossed the border with the 44th on November 30. When the troops were given the order to retreat, the nurses ran for the forests, leaving behind the wounded to freeze to death in the ambulances and in the Finnish farmhouse which they had used as a field hospital. Both other nurses, she explained, were wounded and probably froze to death.

A Russian colonel, a regimental commander from the 44th, was taken prisoner. His captors described him as bald-headed, handsome, with clever eyes and a sad, weary expression. He was not afraid, as were most of the prisoners; his dignity was intact and he spoke slowly, softly, almost to himself as he smoked one cigarette after another. He was lonely because most of his friends, the officers and men, had died on the Raate Road.

During his interrogation he asked the Finns:

For whom was this war, particularly these battles, worthwhile? And for what? Why did these young people have to die? When I was fighting the Czar generals Denikin and Koltshak during the revolution, there was reason to fight. We wanted to give the land to the peasants and the factories to the workers. This is what we did manage. We were fighting for a cause and that is why we won. When we attacked Poland, we wanted to liberate our brothers from oppression. We believed in that cause and again we won. But now that we are sent to Finland, we had no idea of a cause.

I remember being told that we were again on a mission of liberating our worker friends from capitalism, but I do feel in my own skin how we were welcomed by those we came to liberate. What can we possibly offer you Finns that you don't already have? Even though I am a prisoner, I have looked around and have seen a few things that have convinced me that the Finnish worker is better dressed than the Russian Communist official.

I know that Stalin and Voroshilov are clever, sensible men and I can't understand how they were led to this idiotic war. What do we need cold, dark Finland for anyway?

What good soldiers my boys were. They were the best in Russia, the elite division to which my regiment belonged. They were the best in training and weaponry. I remember when my regiment was leaving Leningrad railroad station, the men were telling those who stayed behind, "You fellows will have nothing to do when you get there [Finland]. We'll open the road and we'll meet in Oulu on New Year's Eve.

The colonel was asked about the activities of the 44th Division:

From Murmansk, we marched almost 200 miles in eleven days which I am sure you Finns would have been proud to accomplish. The only thing we received was scolding from headquarters because of our slow march tempo. During this march we began to wonder about the whole war and we certainly knew we were not marching in a parade in the Red Square.

We lost 10 percent of our strength, mainly because of frostbite. . . . When we crossed into Finland we could no longer make campfires because we were assured that bullets and grenades would start dropping in the middle of our camp. Such cold . . . such endless wilderness and darkness. We tried to keep together so we would not get lost. Soldiers crowded shoulder to shoulder in some areas.

The Finns asked why there was no attempt to open the road.

Of course we tried to attack and open the road forward, but it was like hitting your head against a wall. It was different from what we were used to in our previous battles, in Poland, for instance. It was unbelievable . . . awesome.

Our communications didn't work and we began to get hungry.

But Finns we couldn't see anywhere. And believe it or not, the first Finns that I personally saw were the two that took me as a prisoner after my regiment was destroyed. We couldn't see them anywhere, yet they were all over the place. If anybody left the campsite, he met with certain death. When we sent our sentries to take their positions around the camp, we knew that within minutes they would be dead with a bullet hole in the forehead or the throat slashed by a dagger.

This invisible death was lurking from every direction. It was sheer madness. Hundreds, even thousands of my men were slaughtered. . . .

We should personally show Stalin the road that we have taken to Finland, and what happened to us. I think our leaders are concerned about the honor of our Red Army and the ridicule by world opinion. If they are indeed great men, they should not be concerned by what the world thinks of them, but should be concerned about Russia. And Molotov, Zhdanov, and Kuusinen—those provocateurs should come here and dig into the mountains of bodies.

I can't understand how my comrades wound up in these huge piles of bodies anyway. Very, very sad war this is. We Soviets thought that we were respected by other countries because of our peace-loving ways, and the entire civilized world was behind us since we were the cradle of all free workers. Now we are hated and despised. Perhaps this is the result of Molotov policies.

Then the colonel added bitterly, "You'd better bury all those soldiers before spring. Otherwise you'll have a plague."

The Finns who began the defense of their country with practically nothing in the way of weaponry were overwhelmed at their new wealth.

From the 163d, at Likoharju, there were 5 tanks, 35 trucks, 10 motorcycles, 50 horses, and other infantry weapons. At Tyynelä the Finns found 10 tanks, 6 artillery cannons, 42 trucks, 400 live horses, dozens of machine guns and automatic guns. At Haukila, they picked up 40 field artillery pieces, 49 anti-panzer cannon, 13 anti-aircraft machine-guns, 27 tanks, 20 tractors, 160 trucks, and an enormous amount of ammunition and communication equipment.

From the 44th Division the victors collected 46 cannon, 29 panzer cannon, 43 tanks, 200 trucks, 100 machine guns, 190 automatic guns, 6,000 rifles, 1,170 horses.

During the remainder of the war, the Russians were unable to resume the offensive in this sector. The blitzkrieg to cut Finland in half was abandoned after the heavy losses and the Finns could gradually be withdrawn to other fronts.

If the battles of Tolvajärvi and Suomussalmi have been described in detail, it is because, as Mannerheim later wrote, "they were to prove the most remarkable ones from the tactical point of view and because they were of decisive importance for the morale of the Finnish nation. Further, they give the most realistic picture of the pitiless conditions under which the Winter War was fought."

As the new year of 1940 began, the situation for the Russians in Finland was poor. Many of their operations by the middle of December had been stopped along the entire eastern front. Even the Karelian Isthmus was holding. The Russians were suffering heavy casualties in their drive against the Mannerheim Line, and the coldest part of the winter was yet to be faced.

The Finnish army, almost entirely on skis (except at the Karelian

Isthmus), was operating on fourteen main fronts, attacking the heavily armored Russian divisions from the sides and the rear in full confidence of their superiority in this type of warfare.

Both Finnish and Russian military headquarters examined the January scoreboard. Finland's friends in the West looked at it also:

The Russian 14th Army, from Kuollaa sector had sent its 104th Division through Petsamo some 80 miles toward Nautsi village inside Finland, but were forced to withdraw 18 miles. Here they stopped, and there was no further activity.

The Russian 88th Division, which had penetrated some 100 miles inside Finland, was badly beaten and forced back 55 miles from Pelkonsenniemi to Saija where it stopped. Rovaniemi, the main Russian goal for rendezvous, was still some 200 miles away.

The Russian 9th Army, in the Vienan sector, sent its 122d Division against the Finns but soon realized that the enemy was attacking and harassing its rear as well as cutting its supply lines. They were forced to withdraw 20 miles back to Märkä lake.

At the Kuusamo sector most of the Russians were kept on their side of the border. The main force of the 9th Army, the 163d and 44th divisions, were destroyed during the great battles of Suomussalmi-Juntusranta and Raate.

At the Kuhmo sector the Russian 54th Division was almost completely surrounded by the Finns, and their advance was stopped. (Later in January they were encircled and remained there for the duration of the war.)

At Lieksa the Russians were forced to withdraw back behind their own borders after an advance of some 15 miles. Oulu, their goal, was still 170 miles away.

At Ilomantsi the Russian 8th Army sent their 155th Division to Finland, but after December 23 this division was so badly mauled that it could no longer attack. It merely withdrew to more suitable "defensive" positions and stayed there.

At Tolvajärvi and Aittojoki the Russian 139th and 75th divisions were partially destroyed and driven back some 25 miles to the eastern side of the river where they remained in their trenches for the duration of the war.

At Kollaa the Russian 56th and 164th divisions were stopped completely. Their desire for further attacks seemed to have disappeared.

At Käsnäselkä-Salmi Sector the main force of the Russian 8th Army including the 18th and 168th divisions and the 34th Panzer Brigade were some 25 miles inside the Finnish border. Their well-planned operations enabled them to join at Koirinoja and continue their assaults against the Finns near Kitelä-Ruokolake-Ruhtinaanmäki and Syskylake. By early January, however, the defenders had succeeded in taming the Russian troops, so that their desire to advance was no longer there. They finally halted—and dug in.

The 168th Division had moved from Salmi all the way to the fields of Kitelä, some 45 miles from the border, where they were finally stopped, 35 miles short of the city of Sortavala.

The major problem for the Russians along the Finnish frontier seemed to be supplies. As they advanced, they found almost nothing on the Finnish side that they could use for either food or shelter. Everything had been burned by the Finns. The Russian horses were undernourished and often the troops were forced to eat the carcasses of the horses killed in battle; food supplies from the Murmansk Railroad did not arrive on a regular schedule.

As of this date, the Russians were closer to starvation than they knew. Had the Finns succeeded in breaking the Murmansk Railroad somewhere around Lotinanpelto or Petrograd and kept it under their control, no Russian forces inside of Finland would have gotten anything to eat at all. But the Finns were unable to accomplish this feat, so the enemy got food, sometimes.

The start of 1940 saw Finnish headquarters less concerned with matters north of Ladoga. Supplies and weaponry captured on the frozen battlefields would be sent to Karelia . . . while the Russians continued to lose interest in the whole war.

13 | THE *MOTTI* BATTLES

People are talking about *motti* tactics as if the main objective of the Finns was to create them.[1] This is not so. The only one that was planned before the battle was the so-called "great *motti*," in the area of Kitelä-Koirinoja. The smaller nests seemed to form as chips falling this way and that, as the wood carver created his main pieces of art.

> —*Major General J. W. Hägglund,*
> *Commander, 4th Army Corps*

Following their defeat at Raate Road, the commanding general of the Russian 44th Division, Vinogradov; the 662d Infantry commander, Sarov; Commissar Podhomutov; and the commander of the 3d Battalion of the 662d Infantry regiment, Captain Tsaikowski, were all executed by orders from the Soviet High Command. The fate of Major General Selendsov, commander of the 163d Division, is unknown.

The Finnish victor, Colonel Siilasvuo, was promoted to major general and immediately despatched to Kuhmo to seal the fate of the Russian 54th Division.

Before Major General Siilasvuo's arrival at the Kuhmo sector, two Finnish fighting details led by Lieutenant Colonels Ilomäki and Vuokko had harassed the flanks of Major General Gusevski's 54th Division so continuously that the advance had been stopped. Even after the transfer of troops from Lieksa to bolster the 54th, the stranglehold remained firm. More recently the Soviets had sent in Colonel Dolin and perhaps their

[1] *Motti* means approximately a half a cord of chopped wood which woodsmen measure and leave behind at certain distances, to be picked up later. In the Winter War context, it meant an enclave of surrounded enemy troops.

only well-trained ski brigade in the hopes of breaking the Finns' grip on the beleagered division, but 10 miles inside the Finnish border they were surrounded by Finnish skiers at Vetko and Kesseli and destroyed.[2] The future was bleak for the 54th, particularly when Siilasvuo arrived with additional men, artillery, and some twenty mortars, most of which he had confiscated during the Suomussalmi-Raate battles. Siilasvuo was described as being so cocky that he dared to order 3,200 rounds of artillery fire before the main Finnish assaults; an unheard-of luxury anywhere north of Ladoga.

In spite of this pressure, the Russian 54th held its position at the isthmus of Sauna Lake, surrounded by their enemy in a *motti* until they were saved by the peace.

Bearing in mind the Russian training and thinking, the situation developed quite logically. As the fierce battles continued along the various northern roads, the Finns saw the segments of the Russian columns that they had isolated in their pincer maneuvers curling up like worms that had been stepped on. They simply stopped and dug in with their panzers and artillery, and the Finns had no choice but to surround them. Soon Western reporters were telling the world about the Finns' new kind of fighting tactics, but for the Finns, whose real goal was quick destruction of the enemy, *mottis* were a distasteful, though necessary, evil.

The composition of a *motti* depended upon where the Russian column was cut and on what kind of troops and weaponry were isolated. Some groups had only one type of weaponry such as artillery or tanks; others were groups of infantry. Or perhaps these were mixed with the quartermaster corps and their vehicles; sometimes even divisional headquarters were encircled.

Most of the tanks were soon without fuel, but with a good supply of ammunition, their guns could serve as a panzerized defense around the entire belt. The larger *mottis* were extremely powerful with more than enough weapons and ammunition to sustain them indefinitely. Furthermore, the surrounded forces dug in and also built defense fortifications

[2]Khrushchev said, "We tried to put our own troops on skis too. We started intensively to recruit professional sportsmen. We had to bring them from Moscow and the Ukraine as well as from Leningrad. They left in high spirits. Poor fellows were ripped to shreds. I don't know how many came back alive . . . ." Nikita Khrushchev, *Khrushchev Remembers* (Boston: Little, Brown and Company, 1970), p. 153.

of barbed wire and trenches around the perimeter. Although the troops inside did defend themselves with astonishing tenacity, they seldom tried to escape despite the cold and hunger. Meanwhile, a handful of Finns, who soon became bored with their detail, skied around the perimeter periodically to make sure no one escaped.

At first, the surrounded Russians were well supplied with food and ammunition, undoubtedly made available because of their earlier heavy casualties. Due to the Finns' lack of anti-aircraft artillery, Soviet planes could airdrop packages of supplies, and while some of the bundles landed in Finnish hands, the fact that they were dropped at all gave hope to the beleaguered Russians. But as time went on, and days became weeks, the lack of food and material became critical; horsemeat was the daily diet for the unfortunate *motti* populace. Sometimes when one group had exhausted its supplies, it did try to join a larger group nearby, but these attempts ended sadly for the would-be escapees.

Military strategists were puzzled at the passive behavior of the Russians but Mannerheim considered it almost predictable. According to the Red Army manuals and repeated suggestions by high-ranking Red officers, any terrain that had been gained must be kept to the last man. So the Russians held on, starving and freezing to death, trying to keep a flicker of life as long as possible. As a practical matter, they were surrounded by the horrible, terrifying wilderness, and if any men were to venture out without panzer support and artillery, the Finns would simply create another *motti* out of them. Furthermore, any "change of address" at this point would have made the receipt of "airmail" even more unsure.

The Finns did their best to destroy these bases as quickly as possible so they could get on with other jobs, but without heavy weaponry, mortars, and anti-panzer cannon, they were forced to break them up piecemeal. They used their ammunition sparingly, mainly to lower the morale of the surrounded men while night patrol units attacked pillboxes and machine-gun positions along the perimeter. Gradually the "belt" tightened and the circle was narrowed until the end came and the inventory could begin.

This was the "immobile" situation facing General Hägglund in the 4th Army Corp sector. With ten Russian divisions (160,000 troops) packed into a 100-square-mile area, many of which were in a *motti* or in the process of being squeezed into one, strong action had to be taken. The Russians could not be allowed to rest and regroup. The enemy would have to be destroyed.

The plan of operation for the period of January 5–26 called for heavier blows against the divisions which had already been stopped. To deal such heavy blows more men and equipment were needed, and now, with Mannerheim's approval, troops began pouring in. Lieutenant Colonel F. U. Fagernäs, fresh from his victory at Raate Road, arrived with his infantry regiment, the 64th. The 4th Jaeger Battalion, well equipped and experienced after the Karelian Isthmus battles, was moved up to bolster Hägglund's forces. Two guerrilla battalions, the 3d and 4th, arrived while local Home Guard units were searched for younger and older volunteers who would form a new unit. Mannerheim sent from his headquarters Lieutenant Colonel V. K. Nihtilä to assist Hägglund in carrying out the new plans for dealing with ten Russian divisions.

All possible men and materials were scraped together for this crucial phase. Some of the new arrivals were well equipped and experienced; some units still wore their "model Cajander" uniforms (civilian clothes). A few had tents and field kitchens, others had nothing. Even a group from the tenuous positions at Kollaa reported to Hägglund, so that by mid-January the 4th Army Corps had gathered together 46,400 men and 106 cannon.

The prime, emergency goal was to surround the troops of General Bondarev's 168th Division and General Kondrasev's elite 18th Division, along with General Kondratjev's 34th Panzer Brigade, all of whom had joined forces at Kitelä and Ruhtinaanmäki.

The secondary objective was to kill "live" forces, while there was still time.

General Hägglund's forces attacked on January 6, reaching the shores of Lake Ladoga near Koirinoja and Pitkäranta between January 11 and 18. Meanwhile, from the west, other Finnish units arrived at Maksima island, south of Koirinoja. This meant that General Bondarev's 168th Division had no way of making contact with its own forces, other than across the narrow neck of ice toward southeast at Pitkäranta. The trap was closed, like the top of a paper bag. General Hägglund had successfully completed the largest, and only planned, *motti* of the Winter War.

But he still had ten incredibly powerful *mottis* which extended all the way from the Lemetti cross roads to Uomaa village. One by one, he would try to destroy them.

There was Kitelä (the most powerful), the Regiment *motti* nearby, Reponmäki, Koposenselkä, the two *mottis*—East and West Lemetti, Lava lake, Siira road crossing, Uomaa, and Konnunkylä. There were also "unlisted" *mottis* with which to contend. One of these was the so-called Mylly *motti*.

The 4th Jaeger Battalion, fighting in the vicinity of West Lemetti, had been reinforced by a company from the 37th Infantry, led by Captain Väänänen. The 13th Division artillery batteries had been ordered to give the Jaegers their full support. Thus strengthened, the 4th Jaeger was given orders to break up the Mylly *motti*.

Early in the morning of February 2, the battalion commander, Colonel Matti Aarnio, along with a company commander, skied around the Russian nest, hoping to get a view of the underground village. They saw that dugouts had been built side by side, sometimes three "floors" high, with machine guns protruding from the emplacements. Over the village "roofs" tanks had been placed as protective coverings. It was clear that any assault from the outside against such heavily fortified dugouts would be useless; attackers would be needlessly slaughtered.

The Russians spotted the skiing officers and let loose with several rounds of machine-gun bursts. Aarnio said, "Good. Now that we've been seen in the northeast, they'll expect our attack to come from here."

As predicted, the northeast perimeter was promptly reinforced with additional troops while the Finns abandoned any plan to move into that particular area. Instead, they decided to move in on a weak spot near the Kuikka farmhouse; they would send sneak patrols *inside* the *motti* under cover of darkness while the forces outside diverted the enemy's attention by attacking several points simultaneously. Two companies would strike from the east and one from the south; shortly before the assault, all available Finnish artillery would keep the Russians pinned down deep in their dugouts.

The men themselves requested and were granted permission to change their weaponry load before the attack. Instead of carrying heavy rifles which would be useless against panzers anyway, they would fit themselves out with hand grenades, TNT, Molotov cocktails, and submachine guns. Personal handguns such as Mauser pistols were borrowed from machine-gun companies and anti-panzer units.

The first squads sneaked into the *motti* in the cold dark of midnight. One of the older men on the outside commented, "It makes my hair stand on end to know that our men are plunging right into the middle of an enemy *motti!*"

The Finnish intruders moved singly or in pairs, jumping from one protective spot to another. Sometimes they dove into snowbanks and advanced with the camouflage of heavy snow.

The attacking forces outside waited. Everything was quiet.

Now, suddenly, they could see Russian flashlights signaling units inside the *motti*. They were obviously mystified about the activities at their rear —or rather, in their center.

There was the sound of muffled explosions. Only the Finns outside knew what was happening. The Russians were completely bewildered. They undoubtedly wanted to throw hand grenades but they had no idea where to throw them because the Finns had mingled with them in the darkness.

Lieutenant Hahtela, hiding in the Kuikka farmhouse, reported that "destruction of the dugouts has successfully begun."

As later reported, the Finns had set off their TNT charges and tossed their Molotov cocktails and hand grenades while the Russians attempted to frighten the attackers by screaming.

The Finn squads operated freely with little fear of enemy automatic rifle fire because the darkness prevented the Soviets from identifying friend from foe. At 0205 hours, the enemy did manage to get their machine guns into position and the daredevil Finns in their midst were slowed down. At the farmhouse, word was received, "Send more Molotov cocktails!"

The Reds attempted a counterattack, hoping to nail the intruders, but at 0240, they were thrown back. And now the Finns could see the Russians struggling to break the cordon which surrounded them. They screamed and ran in every direction, announcing to the entire *motti* populace the news of the sneak attack on their haven. As they fled, word of their departure was radioed to units guarding the East Lemetti *motti* so the escapees would be pursued.

The hapless men rushed by the hundreds like a tidal wave towards the southeast, leaving behind their panzers, guns, and artillery to plunge blindly into the frozen forest.

At a nearby first-aid station, a Finnish medic and his stretcher-bearer quickly dove into their dugout. The Russian avalanche was streaming towards them and a Finn screamed in Swedish, "They've broken through! Let's get out of here!"

One of the wounded could not be moved, however. So the medic decided to stay with him. Another Finn, at the station, Sergeant Major Grunn, worried about the soldiers' pay which he carried in his pocket, so

(Above left) Marshal Mannerheim. *Courtesy: Defense Ministry, Headquarters Photo Center, Helsinki. (Above right)* Finnish child bundled up and tagged to be sent to Sweden. *Courtesy: Werner Söderström Oy. (Below)* Signing the pact between the Soviet Union and the "People's Democratic Government of Finland" are (left to right) Molotov, Zhdanov, Voroshilov, O. V. Kuusinen (seated), and Stalin. *Courtesy: Werner Söderström Oy.*

The city of Kouvola in southern Finland cleans up after one of the daily Soviet air raids. *Courtesy: Werner Söderström Oy.*

(Above) Hanko, once a prosperous little town, suffered heavily from incendiary bombs. *Courtesy: Werner Söderström Oy. (Below)* Mikkeli, where Mannerheim established his headquarters in an elementary school building, was bombed. *Courtesy: Werner Söderström Oy.*

The Viipuri-Helsinki train carrying women and children was a favorite Russian bombing and strafing target. Often the train stopped and the people ran for the woods. *Courtesy: Werner Söderström Oy.*

(Above) Most of the Finnish air force was made up of 31 Dutch-built Fokker D XXI fighters, which had a blue Lapp ornament, the *hakaristi,* "locked cross," on the wings. This symbol was adopted by Nazi Germany, to become the swastika. *Courtesy: Werner Söderström Oy, Helsinki. (Below)* A shot-down Russian SB bomber on the ice. *Courtesy: Aamulehti, Tampere.*

Lieutenant General Harald Öhquist, Commander of the Finnish 2nd Army Corps (seated), planned the Karelia counterassault. *Courtesy: Defense Ministry, Headquarters Photo Center, Helsinki.*

Colonel Hjalmar Sülasvuo (in white coat) took on the Russian 163rd and 44th divisions at Suomussalmi and Raate Road. *Courtesy: Defense Ministry, Headquarters Photo Center, Helsinki (used by permission).*

(Left) Colonel A. O. Pajari (right), defeated the Russian 139th and 75th divisions at Tolvajärvi. *Courtesy: Defense Ministry, Headquarters Photo Center, Helsinki (used by permission). (Right)* Finnish officers studying the progress and routes of invading Russian divisions. *Courtesy: Institute of Military History, Helsinki.*

General Timoshenko. *Courtesy: Sovfoto.*

At Kollaa was Lieutenant Aarne Juutilainen, known as the "Terror of Morocco" because of his French foreign legion exploits. *Courtesy: Defense Ministry, Headquarters Photo Center, Helsinki.*

The "Northern Finland Group" was led by Major General Viljo Tuompo against the Russian 14th and 9th armies from Kuollaa and Viena. *Courtesy: Otava Publishing Company, Helsinki.*

Corporal Simo Häyhä, the best known Finnish sniper, killed more than 500 Russians. *Courtesy: Defense Ministry, Headquarters Photo Center, Helsinki.*

(Above) The old as well as the young held front line duty, often wearing their "Model Cajander" (civilian) uniforms. Northerners wore *pieksu* boots, home-crafted with turned-up toes that fitted neatly into hand-made leather ski bindings. *Courtesy: Defense Ministry, Headquarters Photo Center, Helsinki. (Below left)* A Finnish captain in the north, wearing his Home Guard uniform, including fur reindeer gloves. The leather cord around his neck is attached to his hand gun to prevent loss. *Courtesy: Defense Ministry, Headquarters Photo Center, Helsinki. (Below right)* A Finnish lieutenant prepares hot coffee in his dug-out. *Courtesy: Werner Söderström Oy.*

(Above) Reindeer were pressed into service at Petsamo in Lapland. *Courtesy: Werner Söderström Oy. (Below)* Russian ski troops discarded their skis before or during battles, while the Finns kept theirs so as to depart quickly after their strikes. *Courtesy: Photo Archives of the Foreign Ministry, Helsinki.*

The Molotov cocktail. The Finns used 70,000 of them, including 20,000 made at the front lines. Finnish guerillas also used TNT, shown at left. *Courtesy: Werner Söderström Oy.*

Finnish cooks, quartermasters, engineers, and riflemen shoved logs or crowbars into the treads of Russian panzers. Crews emerging to make repairs were hit by machine gunners. *Courtesy: Werner Söderström Oy.*

...ig quick-firing Suomi submachine guns, guerilla skiers would suddenly appear, pour bullets ...the Russian masses, and disappear into the whiteness. *Courtesy: Uusi Suomi, Helsinki.*

...ove) Part of the Mannerheim Line "fortress" at the Karelian Isthmus. *Courtesy: Institute ...Military History, Helsinki. (Below)* Finnish wounded had to be treated in fields or forests, ...etimes for days before they could be removed. Medics used *pulkkas*, sleds, to transport ...m. *Courtesy: Aamulehti, Tampere.*

At Kollaa, where the lines were far-flung and the defenders few, single soldiers often dashed to breakthrough points. At "Killer Hill," 4,000 Russians attacked a Finnish platoon of 32 men. *Courtesy: Werner Söderström Oy.*

Women and young boys worked round the clock at munitions factories. *Courtesy: Werner Söderström Oy.*

(Above) Finnish artillery was scarce, often from the Turkish wars and World War I. Shown here is a "modern" artillery piece. *Courtesy: Institute of Military History, Helsinki.* (Right) At Suomussalmi-Raate, light anti-aircraft batteries defended Finnish troops. *Courtesy: Institute of Military History, Hiki, and Werner Söderström Oy.*

Most *mottis* contained tanks, often without fuel. Their guns served for defense around the entire belt. *Courtesy: Werner Söderström Oy.*

Russian heavy equipment at a standstill near the East Lemetti *motti. Courtesy: Werner Söderström Oy.*

Russian prisoners-of-war were cold, hungry, and sick. In some divisions, only 60 percent of the soldiers had been given military training before coming to Finland. *Courtesy: Aamulehti, Tampere.*

Hungry Russian prisoners given their first hot meal since the invasion. *Courtesy: Uusi Suomi, Helsinki.*

At the end, people walked the streets with tears in their eyes. *Courtesy: Werner Söderström Oy.*

As the men returned home from the battlefields, many of them wept at the appalling peace terms. Shown above, the Kuhmo defenders who had successfully *mottied* the elite Russian 54th Division. The Finns still considered themselves an unbeaten army. *Courtesy: Werner Söderström Oy.*

he too stayed in the dugout. Now, even as the Russians were running over their dugout roof, he contacted the Finnish battalion command post with an SOS for help. The reply was, "Too late for help. Get on top of the dugout and fight like heroes!"

The four men readied their hand weapons as the Russians banged on their locked door. There was thumping on the roof and even the smoke-stack was being shaken. Through their observation slot, the Finns could see a Russian soldier killing Lieutenant Salotie's dog, tied to a tree outside. And there was the din of screams and shouts, *"Uraa tovarists!"* The pounding at the door continued as the Finns inside readied their guns and prepared to sell their lives dearly.

But help had been sent. Lieutenant Sareva and his men armed with submachine guns skied to the rescue. The Russians fell into the snow, though some tried desperately to get back to the *motti* which they had just fled from.

While Finn units fought to destroy the remnants of the *motti*, others followed the Russians into the dense timber. Then the entire populace moved out, walking straight ahead into the Finnish machine-gun fire, as if they didn't care any more.

Later, Finns found a few Russians hiding in the farmhouse and in the barn, but by February 4, it was all over for the Mylly *motti*.

The first count of the Russian dead came to 500, but the work details increased that number to 1,000. Among the dead were three Finnish soldiers. The 4th Jaeger Battalion, which was responsible for destroying the Mylly *motti*, lost only five of its men.

One by one, the *mottis* fell. And even the Finns were deeply moved by the sadness and desperation of the messages they intercepted. They had continually said in their propaganda messages, "Go back to Russia, leave Finland alone," but at this point, the Russians could go nowhere, forward or back. All they could do was call for help. And the tighter the Finns squeezed them into their *mottis*, the more numerous were the messages.

From East Lemetti on February 24 at 5:38 P.M. came the message: "Finnish artillery and anti-panzer fire has caused us heavy casualties. Since 19 February, 12 tanks, 2 armored cars and 42 trucks have been destroyed. Please fire heavy artillery against the Finnish positions north of Lemetti and Mitro. Please support us. The Finns are only 200 yards away from our positions."

At 6:00 P.M. that same day there was another message from the group.

"Please airdrop food and supplies, regardless of weather. Last drop did not include ammunition. Please air drop ammunition. Two days without bullets. Food and fodder all gone. Try to send some today. Why do you let us suffer without food and fodder? Please do something about it!"

The pleas of the encircled men continued. "Why don't you attack immediately from about 200 to 300 yards? Attack at 1239 hours. Four aircraft did not drop any food at all. Generally we received too little food. The greater portion landed on the Finnish side."

1241 hours: "Detail Petrova has been completely destroyed. Expecting reinforcements. I am requesting reinforcements which should arrive in the morning."

1800 hours: "Why don't you answer our messages? Do you have contact with Army Corps headquarters?"

On February 26 at 2100 hours, the Finns intercepted a message sent to the 34th Panzer Brigade from the Russian LVI Army Corps: "We are aware of your difficult position, and we have informed Stern and Kovalev about it. We are making plans to assist you with air support."

The 34th Panzer Brigade answered, "Please inform us quickly of the location of the Finnish left flank at Kuikka [farmhouse]. And what is happening at Lava Lake?"

As the various *mottis* were broken up and destroyed, many prisoners of war said that their own troops in the darkness accidentally shot each other. "The only hero is the one who doesn't give himself up."

The Russian soldiers were hungry in their *mottis* but their horses which were supposed to pull their cannon and supply wagons were even worse off. They were tragic shadows almost from the beginning of the invasion, so by the time they were entrapped, the poor beasts were useless save as food for the starving soldiers. The logistics of feeding the large force of Russian horses on land that had been purposely scorched by the defenders was staggering. According to the Finnish manuals, a horse requires about 26 pounds of fodder per day. This would mean some 1,261 tons of fodder per day, and four trainloads per day for transport. The Russians had made no plans for feeding their horses on so grand a scale.

Red Army horses that did not starve to death or were not slaughtered for food sometimes served other purposes. Near Koirinoja the Russians used them to "neutralize" Finnish mines by driving the animals back and forth across the explosive ice fields. The Finns, seeing the terrible suffering of the horses, tried to shoot them before they hit the mines. Sometimes they were able to kill them before they were wounded; other times they were forced to witness the agonized moans of the injured beasts as they suffered for hours on end.

Erkki Palolampi, who had been a newspaper editor in civilian life, kept a diary of his experiences at the front. In it he describes an incident on a day when the "cavalry without riders" were driven over the ice. A horse was badly wounded near the Finnish lines; its cries and moans sounded almost human. The Finns wanted to end its suffering, but with the weather clear and the enemy's guns well in place, such a mission would be suicidal. The commanding officer forbade anyone to leave his position. Tension mounted and the battalion that had seen so much suffering and death was now beginning to shake and lose its nerve because of one wounded animal on the ice. Cold sweat broke out on the men's foreheads. Something had to be done.

Pastor Eljas Simojoki, the chaplain who had been with the battalion since Savolaska, stepped forward. He was the man who had said the last prayers for the dying or bandaged the wounded and carried them to safety. Since there was no formally designated Chaplain's Corps during the Winter War, he also fought along with the combatants. Everyone loved Simojoki. He had always followed orders—until now.

The pastor picked up his hand gun and walked calmly over the wide white space of snow and ice. No shot was fired from either side and it was clear that everyone wanted the horse put out of its misery.

Simojoki reached the horse and did his merciful deed. The horse became quiet and the pastor began the long walk back. The silence was absolute.

The enemy waited until Simojoki reached his own lines before opening their fire to kill him.[3]

As General Hägglund well knew, the Russians, during the early days of January, were busily reorganizing and regrouping their forces. A new army (the 15th) was formed under the leadership of Marshal G. M. Stern who in August, 1939, had distinguished himself during the ten-day battle at the Khalka River against the Japanese. The 8th Army headquarters was

---

[3]Finnish horses fared well in the Winter War. They had good food and stabling, with veterinarian service which was the best in any war in history. These horses became very clever about lying down during artillery bombardment or aircraft attacks. Finnish farmers later complained that their plow horses continued to lie down in peacetime when civilian airlines flew over their fields.

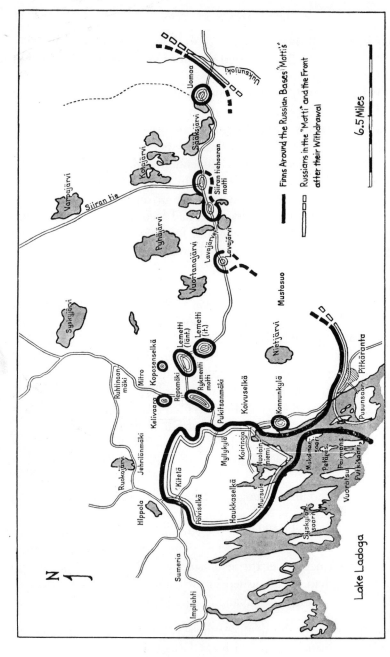

Uomaa, Siira Road crossing, Lavalake, East Lemetti, West Lemetti, Regiment, Repomaki, Koposenselkä, Konnunkylä and Kitelä Great *motties* during the *motti* battles north of Lake Ladoga in the Winter War. *Courtesy: Werner Söderström Oy, Helsinki, Finland*

transfered to Karhumäki and the LVI Army Corps commander, Tšerepanov, moved his headquarters from Käsnäselkä, so as to be nearer the 168th Division. This proved to be a sad decision, because Tšerepanov soon found himself surrounded in a *motti* at Koirinoja. From then on, his headquarters ceased to function.

On February 8 another Russian army corps was formed near Salmi. The VII Corps commanded by General Korotajev was a new, fresh force brought into the area in the hope that it would change the course of events for the Russians.

Meanwhile, the terrible and bloody battles continued. Colonel Matti Aarnio experienced the last desperate attempts of the Russians to escape from the East Lemetti panzer *motti*.

As commander of the 4th Jaeger Battalion, he had received a message from the forward observation post that hundreds of Russians were breaking out of their trap and were heading towards his battalion campsite along the supply road. They were now only a few hundred yards away. Aarnio immediately ordered all communications cut and everyone around the post to head for the campsite. Masses of Russians passed the defense positions of Lieutenant Sareva and Lieutenant Sorvali while Finnish units opened fire against the oncoming infantry. The Russians began falling by the dozens, but still being outnumbered, the Finns were forced out of their positions.

The Russians were now twenty yards away and Aarnio was able to determine that these troops were led by a large group of high-ranking officers. General Kondratjev and his headquarters office were desperately trying to get out of the *motti*. Only a few hours earlier Aarnio had been assured that this area was free of enemy troops so he had dispersed his forces to various points around the perimeter. Now, faced with the onslaught of the escaping Russians, he hastily prepared a defense line made up of his office personnel; messengers, office boys, cooks, and drivers.

Among the prisoners brought into the command post were many men who spoke fluent Finnish. It was soon learned that the men were Russian Karelians and it was sad for the Finns to know they were actually fighting their own kinsmen. "There are at least 3,600 infantry soldiers attempting to get out," Aarnio was told.

By this time the battle sounds at the campsite had been heard by the Finnish patrols who had been sent earlier to encircle the trapped forces. They rushed back to the scene of the breakthrough and poured murderous fire on the fleeing enemy. The entire scene was chaos and confusion. Men shot their own troops in the melee. The battalion clerk ran into the command post to report that the Russians were already outside the camp. When he turned to leave, he was hit at the doorway. Aarnio ran outside to see his new recruits and headquarters company men forming a chain near the command tent. "Don't shoot your own! Wait until you see the Russians!" he shouted.

Fifty more Finns arrived at the command post to take their positions. Sergeant Rastas showed up with twenty-seven communications men. Aarnio quietly commented, "So these are my reserves!"

"Take positions to the south of the camp!"

The sounds of the battle echoed from so many different directions that it was impossible to keep track of what was going on. But within an hour or so, most of the fleeing Russians had stopped shooting. The surprised Finns climbed out of their hastily chosen positions only to see hundreds of dead Russians on both sides of the supply road and in the surrounding forest.

Aarnio, and several of his headquarters officers, inspected the bloody battlefield. The sight was unbelievable. In an area 250 yards along the roadside 400 Russians lay dead, some in layers of three. They had carried nothing with them except hand weapons. There were no tanks, no artillery, no machine guns in this last frantic effort.

Among the dead was the commander of the 34th Panzer Brigade, General Stepan Ivanovitch Kondratjev and all of his headquarters officers including four women typists. Dead, too, were commanding Gen. Kondrašev, the officers of the 18th Division, the artillery commander of the LVI Army Corps, Colonel Bolotov, and the artillery commander of the 18th Division, Colonel Glogorov. In all, 310 high-ranking officers were sprawled alongside their 112 enlisted personnel.

These were not the dirty, poorly-dressed officers seen in earlier campaigns, but instead all were clean and wearing white shirts under their well-tailored uniforms. They were a different class altogether, more like a peacetime parade group. Here was the Moscow elite—a far cry from the other linemen, most of whom came from Soviet Karelia.

Among the Finnish dead were Lieutenants Salotie and Merjamo who lay next to each other just twenty yards ahead of the Russian bodies. Five other headquarters company NCOs lost their lives fighting the enemy break-out which left 3,000 Russians dead. This was the end of the East Lemetti panzer *motti*.

Later that evening, a wounded Russian battalion commander, Captain Gulutki from the Moscow district, was brought into the command tent. All was quiet except for the sounds of Soviet aircraft flying overhead. Aarnio discussed the day's events and the men who had fallen in battle. During the conversation, the Russian fell asleep; when he awoke, Aarnio apologized for not sending him to the first-aid station.

"Your own aircraft would most likely shoot you on the way," the Finn explained. "I will arrange for transport later tonight."

"Thank you," the Russian said. "You are showing me great consideration."

Aarnio said, "We handle all P.O.W.s the same way, regardless of rank. An enemy soldier who has surrendered is no longer an enemy. He is a human being."

The Russian captain replied, "I have seen today a lot of wonderful things about you Finns and my opinion of the brave Finnish army has changed completely."[4]

The quantity of material captured after the battle at East Lemetti was the largest from all the *mottis* except Kitelä: 105 tanks, 12 armored cars, 237 trucks, 31 regular sedans, 10 tractors, 6 heavy artillery pieces, various artillery wagons, 30 field kitchens, 3 mine sweepers (land), 231 other horse-drawn wagons, and 200 carloads of ammunition. The stacks of infantry weapons and piles of other material were counted at a later time.

During this period, General Hägglund's 4th Army Corps destroyed all of the *mottis* except those at Kitelä, Siira crossroads, and Uomaa. Hägglund issued orders to discontinue further attacks and to simply keep the enemy pinned down in these areas (which were finally saved by the peace).

"With this campaign," wrote Mannerheim, "the situation on the long Eastern front had become stabilized and severe defeats had been inflicted on the adversary in all sectors. Unfortunately, this did not permit the Finns to release sufficient troops in time for the battle in the main theater of war, which in the beginning of February had entered into a decisive phase."

[4]This account is based on events in *Talvi Sodan Ihme* [The Miracle of the Winter War] (Jyväskylä, Finland: K. J. Gummerus, 1966), pp. 374–78.

14 | TIMOSHENKO'S OFFENSIVE

Stalin was frantic over the news from the Finnish front. The big debut of the Red Army was still failing miserably, despite fresh troops and new equipment pouring into the battle zones. Western newspaper headlines called full attention to the Finn successes along with the Russian losses and on December 31, 1939, the German General Staff produced their evaluation of their ally's performance:

"In quantity, a gigantic military instrument. . . . Organization, equipment and means of leadership unsatisfactory—principles of leadership good; leadership itself, however, too young and inexperienced. Communication system bad, transportation bad, troops not very uniform; no personalities—simple soldiers, good natured, quite satisfied with very little. Fighting qualities of the troops in heavy fighting, dubious. The Russian 'mass' is no match for an army with modern equipment and superior leadership."[1]

With the apparent inability of the Western powers to agree even in principle on how best to invade Scandinavia in order to secure Sweden's iron ore and Norway's ports, and with Russia's deadlock in Finland, Hitler's admirals urged immediate action. On January 13, 1940, Hitler ordered a military committee to research the feasibility of military action in the north, with an eye to the Norwegian ports of Narvik and Trondheim for use by Admiral Karl Dönitz's U-boat force. Operating under the code name Research N, it was the birth of the so-called Weser War

[1] *Nazi Conspiracy and Aggression* (Washington, 1946), VI, pp. 981–82.

Maneuvers—the attack on Norway and Denmark on April 9, 1940.

Meanwhile, the Western powers were pressuring Finland, insisting that aid be accepted at once. The British were prepared to take over Norwegian ports as well as Sweden's mines and steel mills while at the same time sending at least a brigade into Finland. This, according to General Edmund Ironside, Chief of the Imperial General Staff, would justify the presence of the Allies in Scandinavia. The mines, along with the cities of Bergen and Stavanger, should be occupied no later than March 20 in order to beat Hitler to the punch. Ironside advocated the use of at least five divisions, along with two bomber and two fighter squadrons for this purpose. Protestation of Norwegian and Swedish neutrality fell on deaf ears, even though Swedish representatives pointed out that German bombers would destroy most of their cities before the Allies could bring in additional forces. "When great powers are waging war, small countries can't afford to be heroic," they said.

With this kind of intrigue in the wind, Stalin knew there was no time to lose. Finland must be beaten to her knees, regardless of the cost.

The Soviet premier rearranged the entire leadership of his armies attacking Finland; many of the commanders were either shot or replaced. Marshal K. E. Voroshilov, people's commissar of defense, was demoted to deputy chairman of the Defense Council of the Soviet government. Marshal Semyon K. Timoshenko, who up to that point had been the commander of the North Caucasian, Kharkov, and Kiev Military Districts and who also had taken part in the occupation of Poland in September, became commander of the entire Finnish campaign and the new people's commissar of defense. In particular, he was to mastermind the Karelian Isthmus breakthrough. General Meretskov, who had previously commanded all Russian forces in Finland, was demoted to lead only the 7th Army at the West Isthmus. General Grondahl, a former artillery colonel from the czar's army who was of Swedish-Finnish parentage, would hold the reins of the Red's 13th Army at the East Isthmus.

As Marshal Mannerheim had anticipated, the Russians selected as their breakthrough point an area east of Summa village in the west Karelian Isthmus. Here the fields were large and open and the Russians could use their heavy concentrations of tanks and infantry. Even heavy snow drifts would not prevent panzers from piercing the Finnish defense lines.

Timoshenko's plans were well prepared. Numerous additional divisions were brought into the West Isthmus area and the 13th Army joined the Russian forces in the eastern area. While this was going on, the Russians busied themselves with continuous smaller assaults aimed at wearing down the already exhausted Finns. Heavy artillery constantly pounded the Finns at their positions and by the beginning of February, Marshal Timoshenko had concentrated twenty-five divisions against the Mannerheim Line.

Meanwhile, according to Khrushchev, Stalin was gnashing his teeth in Moscow, waiting for the news that his "engines" had settled matters, once and for all. "Our air force has been called into action. Many bridges have been destroyed. Many trains have been crippled." Stalin then pointed out, "The Finns have only their skis left. Their supply of skis never runs out."[2]

On February 1, 1940, the blanket bombing of the Finnish rear forces by the Soviet air force heralded the beginning of the end for the stubborn Finns. Massed for the attack were some 600,000 Soviet troops, including Timoshenko's well-seasoned Ukrainian forces. Huge masses of artillery lined up hub to hub to rain fire and steel on the Mannerheim Line. In a single twenty-four hour period, no less than 300,000 shells fell on the Summa positions. It was the most massive barrage since the German shelling of the French at Verdun in World War I. At Summa and Lähde the artillery was so heavy that the Russians resorted to the seldom used tactic, the rolling barrage. They simply increased and decreased their range without shifting the fire. Finnish reconnaissance planes reported that in front of Summa, in one sector alone which was about 1.3 miles wide, a total of 104 enemy batteries with their 440 cannon were pounding at the Finns, who had only 16 batteries. The Finnish artillery was of smaller caliber and had a much shorter range than that of the Russians. And the Finns were fast running out of ammunition.

At the Hatjalahti lake and the Muolaa lake sectors, an area 16 miles wide, the Russians attacked with six divisions and 500 aircraft. Enemy infantry, protected by smoke screens and supported by 28- and 45-ton tanks, advanced in regimental and battalion strength. They came in massive waves, testing the Finn defenses and sometimes penetrating the line. But the Finns managed to push them back with their nightly counterassaults. This activity continued for days as fresh Russian troops passed through the carnage of entire divisions which had preceded them.

It was apparent from the way artillery fire was cleverly adapted to the movements of the infantry that the Russians had at last learned to orches-

---

[2]Nikita Khruschev, *Khruschev Remembers* (Boston: Little, Brown and Company, 1970), p. 155.

"I had no idea when I was a kid that it would be so much fun to be a grown-up."
Cartoonist: Jussi Aarnio. Published by Linnoittaja. *Used by permission, Oy Lehmus, Tampere, Finland.*

trate the co-operation between the different arms of their forces. Nevertheless, even after a week, the main defenses of the Mannerheim Line were nowhere near broken. But the fighting men of Finland, who had no more replacements, were dog-tired. Worse, they were nearly out of ammunition; weaponry they had confiscated earlier required Russian ammunition they did not have.

On February 6 the final Russian offensive began. Three divisions with 150 tanks aimed their assault along a 5-mile front while 200 Soviet airplanes bombed the defense line. The enemy's initial successes were quite meaningless, however; their losses were tremendous as Finnish machine gunners in their pillboxes mowed them down in windrows. Thousands of dead Russians lay in front of the Finnish dugouts while fresh troops charged over the frozen bodies. The fact that the Red Army did not count

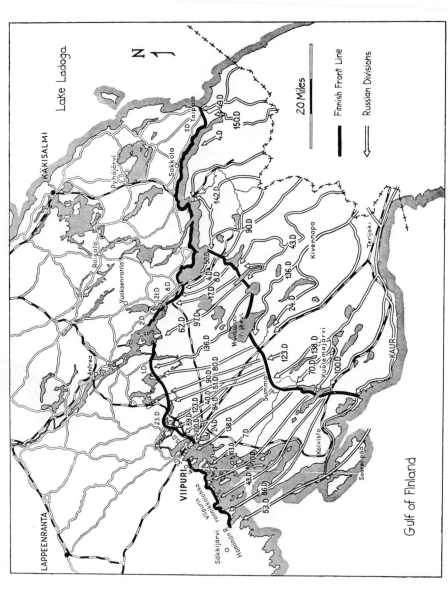

Russian breakthrough at Karelian Isthmus in February 1940 *Courtesy: Werner Söderström Oy, Helsinki, Finland*

its dead relieved the leaders and their consciences of the responsibility and mistakes of this pitiless way of fighting a war. This same day fifty Russian panzers were put out of action.

On February 7 enemy troops penetrated the region of Muolaa, while at the same time they struck twice at Summa. The following day, new fresh Russian troops attacked the 3d Division again and broadened the assault to the 2d Division's sector and on the ninth they were hitting at the 4th Division.

By February 11 the Russians were fighting the entire 2d Army Corps and attempts were made to turn the Finnish flanks at the Gulf of Finland and at Lake Ladoga by crossing over the ice, using tanks, infantry, and cavalry. At 8:20 A.M. the heaviest artillery barrage of the entire war began. One hundred batteries, aimed mainly at Lähde, tore the defense line to bits. Machine-gun bases vanished; everything was blasted to ruin.

The defenders fought bravely, but they were unable to prevent the tanks from rolling over their trenches as the Russian infantry poured through the breaks.

The seriously drained Finnish forces were unable to counterattack successfully. Many of them were so tired that even the roar of the Russian panzers couldn't keep them awake. Their casualties were extremely heavy. The strikes to patch up the Lähde break continued through the night into the early morning, but in the predawn hours, the Russian blows fell again on Summa-Suokanta and Lähde. The fighting raged all day; by now, even Finnish quartermasters and cooks were in the front lines. Most of their battalions were down to one-half to one-third of their regular strength. Untrained, inexperienced recruits and older men activated from Home Guard garrisons and units were sent directly to the front and into combat. Such immediate contact with the enemy was usually disastrous for the beginners, so that these forces were being hopelessly depleted. The Russians could replace their dead and wounded with fresh troops, but the Finns finally had no more to send into action.

With the grave situation at the Mannerheim Line, all available troops were sent to the Karelian Isthmus from north of Ladoga and Lapland. Since the situation at Lähde could no longer be stabilized, Marshal Mannerheim personally arrived at the scene on February 14 to study the matter. He decided that the old defense positions on the Karelian Isthmus would have to be left to the enemy. The Finns would have to withdraw to their weaker, multiple-line defense positions some 2 to 10 miles back.

The Russians made no attempt to pursue the Finns; the withdrawal progressed without any notice. In some places the Russians approached the Finnish trenches after heavy artillery shelling and found the trenches empty. In another sector the Russians, in their jubilation, climbed on top of what was left of the Finnish bunkers and planted a Soviet flag. An angry Finn cleared the peak of the bunker with his submachine gun, jumped on top of it, and threw the flag to the ground.

But the Russians were moving forward at long last. There was good news to report to the newly-appointed people's commissar of defense yet strangely enough it was hard to convince Moscow that the Red Army's bludgeoning of the Mannerheim Line was succeeding. N. N. Voronov, chief marshal of artillery, explains the situation:

On February 15 the hurricane of our bombs and shells descended on Summa. I was at a forward observation post. After the artillery had shifted its fire to the required depth, infantry and tanks simultaneously attacked and began to advance successfully. This time the enemy did not hold out. His flanks were in danger of encirclement, and he began to retreat.

The strongpoint fell before my eyes. Upon returning to the command post of the 7th Army, I witnessed a telephone conversation between Meretskov and the People's Commissar of Defense. No one in Moscow would believe that our troops had captured Summa. Upon seeing me, Meretskov spoke into the telephone:

"Comrade People's Commissar, Voronov has just come in. He saw everything with his own eyes."

I gave a detailed report of the course of the battle to the People's Commissar. Nonetheless, he asked me three times if the report that the strongpoint had been taken was true.

Finally his irritated tone became warm and friendly. The People's Commissar wished the troops a successful completion of this offensive."[3]

The Finns began their withdrawal from their main defense positions on the West Isthmus on February 16. The heavy bombs that the Russians had dropped behind their lines had cut their roads to bits. New roads were quickly built so that equipment could get through. As for the men, there was so much sand and debris in the area that many were unable to move, even on skis. Bridges were constructed over the bomb craters that were sometimes more than 10 feet deep and 54 feet wide—the width of a country road. When they were finally able to proceed, they left behind them small units to harass the advancing Russian troops.

With the withdrawal came an emergency shake-up of the Finnish

[3]N. N. Voronov, *Na sluzhbe voennoi* (Moscow, 1963), pp. 153–57.

commands. On February 19, Lieutenant General Erik Heinrichs, well-known scholar, military expert, and diplomatic troubleshooter, was named commander of all Karelian Isthmus forces, replacing General Österman whose wife, Marga, had been invalided during the air bombardments; Österman himself also pleaded illness because of the exhausting Karelian command. Replacing Heinrichs as 3d Army Corps commander was recently promoted Major General Talvela. The 2d Army Corps defending the West Isthmus was divided into two sections; the newly created 1st Army Corps was led by Major General Laatikainen.

With the Finns in their new temporary defense lines, the Russians began fighting with a sense of victory. For them the war was all but over. But not for the Finns who were still fighting back.

At Mustalampi the Finns destroyed an entire battalion, along with five tanks. Between February 20 and 22 some 800 Russians were killed and the Finns confiscated their 29 machine guns; at Salmenkaita the Russians lost 400 men and 15 machine guns. Between February 20 and 24 the Finnish 1st Division destroyed 18 tanks and collected 38 machine guns and some 280 rifles. The loss of enemy tanks averaged from ten to thirty a day. Finnish optimists began talking about the possibility that the Russians had lost every one of their tanks; some even sat down and figured that the Russians would soon be pressing for peace.

But inch by inch the Finns were withdrawing. Their front line was like a basket full of holes, leaking here and now there, and the leaks could no longer be patched. Sometimes the Russian panzers ventured behind the Finnish lines without any infantry support at all. But once there, they didn't know what to do; when darkness fell, "death would be knocking on their panzer doors." If the Russians were forced to stay overnight in their tanks, they formed a circle and fired their guns periodically in all directions.

Until February 18 the Viipuri inlet had been defended by two battalions under navy command. Now this sector was released to the Karelian army. Additional troops were transferred from Lapland, and on February 28 the so-called Viipuri coastal sector was formed under the command of Major General Wallenius. The fierce battles continued in the temporary and intermediate defense positions between February 17 and 26, and all other assaults were repelled except at Näykki lake where the enemy was successful in breaking through. A recently formed 23rd Division composed mainly of older reservists found itself in tremendous difficulties.

The Russians again moved out on the ice and threatened the Finnish right flank, regardless of the Finns' attempts to keep open their anti-tank water ditches. It was a hopeless task in such extreme cold. The enemy was already attacking, on February 22, the Uuraa Islands in the Viipuri inlet, and the Finns at Koivisto began to withdraw across the ice to the west shore of the inlet. The enemy breakthrough at Näykki lake continued to expand; the Finns were forced to leave their hastily prepared positions and go back to the line of Viipuri-Tali-Naatala-Kaltovesi-Vuoksi. Many of the battles on the islands near Viipuri were fought almost to the last Finn. Only a few men were able to make it back to their own lines in the darkness.

Meanwhile, on February 26, the Finns in desperation decided to use their tanks on the battlefield. Thirteen light Vickers, calling themselves the 4th Detached Panzer Company, received orders to support the 3d Infantry Battalion in a counterattack against the Russians who had broken through the lines between Honkaniemi and Näykkijärvi.

The assault began at 6:30 A.M., but only one company of the 3d Battalion could move forward; the other two companies were left behind with heavy casualties they had suffered during the first phases. Only seven of the Vickers tanks continued to be operational.

By 9:00 the Finns' counterattack was at a complete standstill. The heavy Russian infantry and their many tanks and anti-panzer cannon were too tough to break through. Three Finnish tanks gallantly made it all the way to the Russian lines where they were destroyed. The attack was a complete failure.

Two days later the Finns at the Karelian Isthmus witnessed a Russian tragedy. The enemy had opened with massive artillery preparation and the Finns were now waiting for the inevitable attack. But it did not come. A Finnish officer later described what happened:

All through the day we heard voices from no-man's-land. They were voices of men in pain, and we saw some Russians crawling on the ground back and forth and suddenly the voices were quiet [the Finns had fired their artillery and mortar]. Then one single voice began screaming, "Stalin, Stalin, Stalin!" It was awesome in the otherwise quiet night. It was clear that the Russian soldier had gotten stuck in our barbed-wire fences and we decided that if the Russians were coming to rescue the man we would let them do it. But nobody came. Since we did not want to send any of our own men, a quick machine-gun burst was fired at the man and the screaming stopped.

The following night two Finnish patrols went to check the area but found only dead Russians. When daylight came, the mystery was cleared up when Finnish patrols again went to the scene and verified the report of the night patrol. The bodies of 400 men covered an area of two acres so that they were almost side by side. Many of them had pieces of bread in their hands and had been eating when they were killed. It was now clear that the Russian artillery fire of the night of the twenty-eighth had been about one kilometer short and had landed, not on the Finns, but on a fresh battalion only recently arrived at the front. They were only some 200 meters from the Finnish positions and were planning to encircle, but in the two-hour Russian artillery preparation, every last man had been killed. Even their artillery observer was found in a sitting position, still clutching his map and telephone receiver. Perhaps he had been killed early in the barrage and could not alert the Russian batteries of their error. The firing had been done by 16- and 18-inch guns, the heaviest on the front. One man had been cut in half with the top part of his body landing on another man's neck; they remained in an upright position. A dead lieutenant colonel held an open bread box and some canned goods in his lap, along with a bottle of vodka.

Later information revealed that this Russian battalion had just been graduated from the Leningrad noncommissioned officers' school, and had perhaps been dining in Leningrad restaurants just two days before. Most of the men were about twenty-two or twenty-three years old, good-looking, and wearing new uniforms cut from silk and wool fabric. All wore new flannel underwear. Their faces were clean and shaven and none had been affected by the cold. There were several captains, first lieutenants, and NCOs.

The Finnish officer who viewed the scene said: "The map cases were full of maps and papers. We found hastily printed copies of Finnish positions including every pillbox, dugout, and trench. Red arrows indicated the direction of their planned attack . . . Snow was falling lightly, but the enemy was quiet. Only a few grenades traveled at intervals above us."

The quartermasters with horses worked at picking up war material from the battalion throughout the day. The first sleds brought in twelve new machine guns. They were painted white, and almost all of them had their original factory lubricants. Besides these weapons there were rifles, more machine guns, and everything a battalion carries with it into battle.

Handguns did not wind up in the sleds, because the Finns filled their own pockets with these badly needed weapons.

The dead carried with them unusually large amounts of paper money and silver. By late afternoon of that day almost the entire trench walls of the Finns were covered with Russian paper money, most of which wound up in the mud.

Soviet Major General Minjuk boasted in the Ogonek newspaper on February 25, 1941:

The breakthrough against the Mannerheim Line holds the highest place in all times in the history books for bravery, military ability and examples of war tactics. Difficult terrain, forests, swamps, lakes, added to the strength of the Defense Line made it stronger than any other European fortress. The Red Army was the first one in history that could have made such a brave breakthrough of the fortress. The honor belongs to the Red Army from now on.

15 | THE TERRIBLE DECISION

The Finns were tired. After suffering some 30,000 casualties during the past month, their lines were thin. Artillery was so scarce that cannon had to be shifted from one sector to another. Because of the lack of ammunition, the 2d Army Corps, which was under the heaviest pressure, was allowed only two or three rounds per cannon. Orders were that the front line troops could ask for artillery support only if the target was at least of battalion strength. Under such conditions, the outnumbering enemy had no problem finding soft spots in the Finnish defense line. Weakness was everywhere, and the Russians only had to push their never-ending supply of fresh troops through the breaking points.

Even as the Finns were withdrawing from the west Karelian Isthmus, the enemy divisions, having occupied Teikarsaari and Tuppura, launched an attack across Viipuri inlet on March 2 and managed to get a foothold at Häränpää and Vilaniemi areas. The Finns were successful at first in repelling the attack, but by March 5 and 6, the sector was firmly in Russian hands. But with Finnish reinforcements sent to this area from other fronts, the Russians were not directly, at this point, threatening to cut the roads leading west from the city of Viipuri.

The heaviest battles were now raging at the Tali area where the enemy succesfully broke the flimsy defense positions on March 8 and managed to cross the Tali river. Around Vuosalmi the Russians succeeded in securing the east shore of the Vuoksi river.

In spite of these Finnish reverses, there was no major panic or chaos developing on any front at the Karelian Isthmus. Nevertheless, Mannerheim's headquarters was planning a withdrawal to as far back as the Luumäki Line. And while the peace negotiations were already taking place, it was reasoned that the Finns would be in a somewhat better bargaining position in the more secure location. The exhausted Finnish army was still holding its own around Viipuri.

Meanwhile, Marshal Mannerheim and the Defense Council continued to remind the Finnish government that the need for men and guns was desperate. He recommended peace first, and aid from Sweden as a second choice, but it must come soon. As a last resort, Finland should accept aid from the Western Allies, even though by now it was known that help to Finland was of secondary importance in the scheme of things. The Finnish Cabinet was divided as to what should be done.

Only the week before the French had informed Finland that 50,000 troops were ready to be sent through Narvik and Petsamo. Another 50,000 British were ready to go. Said Daladier and Chamberlain, as late as March 12: "We are waiting for the Finnish request. If we only get the word that we are in agreement with the Finnish government's request and wishes, we will send the troops along."

But the Finns were skeptical. Of this force of 100,000 British and French troops, only a token would reach Finland while the rest would remain to secure strategic Scandinavian positions against the projected German attacks.

The first strike force offered by the French would consist of one Alpine brigade, one Polish brigade, and two battalions from the French foreign legion. The British, who would lead the landing at Narvik and Trond-heim, would send their 42d and 44th divisions. Would not these troops fare as badly as the Russians in the northern wilderness? Airplanes and pilots, yes, because they would not be confronted with the heavy snow and thick forests that faced ground troops. No elaborate supply systems would be needed other than fuel and airplane maintenance, and considering the heavy Russian concentrations, even a few squadrons would be of great help. Unhappily, sufficient air power was not offered.

There were other considerations. If the Finns accepted Western aid and turned down Moscow's offer of a settlement, the entire Scandinavian peninsula would become a major theater in the nearly global war, with Germany possibly entering on the side of Russia. A totally different world situation would develop with a Nazi-Soviet alliance against a Western Allied front extending from the Arctic Circle to the Mediterranean, and beyond. France was especially anxious for the localized northern conflict to become a part of the larger combat area. Many Finns reasoned that this new aid to them was not merely for the sake of their pretty blue eyes.

The more generous the assistance promised, the greater their hesitancy to accept it, since the complexity it involved now seemed worse than the terms offered by the Russians.

But the Allies continued to coax the Finns into resisting Moscow's terms. They promised to exert pressure on Sweden and Norway for transit permission, but this brought up the unpleasant aspects of public opinion. Norway and Sweden would thus be forced into the war, and would they not later blame Finland for involving them? Would they not ask, "Were Viipuri and Sortavala really necessary to keep your Finnish independence?"

It was a terrible decision for any government to make, particularly in view of the people's sacrifices. Should Finland ally herself with the West or must she succumb to the East?

The matter was further complicated when P. E. Svinhufvud, former president of Finland, accompanied by two other men, took off on a self-appointed mission to Berlin. Unknown to the Finnish government, he pleaded Finland's case directly with Hitler. He then went on to Rome where he did the same with Mussolini. His venture was a fiasco, and extremely embarrassing to the Finnish government.

Everyone seemed to have something to say about the war; how to continue it—or how to end it. Germany advised Finland to terminate the hostilities and give in to the Soviets. Wigert von Blücher, the German minister in Helsinki, denied any aid to Russia but hinted that perhaps Finnish and Russian negotiators might meet in Berlin to settle their differences. This suggestion seemed unsuitable to the Finns. The matter lay at rest, with Germany's threat that the war would be extended to the Scandinavian peninsula if Finland accepted Allied aid.

The Allies, promising three and a half divisions to support the Finnish side, were now prepared to prevent all shipments of ore leaving Sweden and southern Russia from reaching Germany.

The Finns asked Sweden to mediate between the Russians and themselves. They were ready to give up Hanko if it would only bring peace, but the Soviet terms were as harsh as ever and the Finns felt they could not accept. But what could they do?

The Foreign Affairs Committee of the Cabinet asked Sweden once more if she would allow transit facilities to Western Allied troops to Finland. Marshal Mannerheim asked the United States to serve as mediator since Sweden seemed to be so absorbed in her desire to remain neutral. He also suggested that Russia might be offered territorial compensation in the north and in the Åland Islands instead of in the southern part of Finland. This too "fell into the sand."

On March 5 the deadline arrived for the Finns' decision. True, their front lines were in critical shape, but with twelve new French and fifty British bombers ready to take off, maybe they could hold out a while longer. At this point Stockholm again informed Helsinki that the Cabinet had decided, by unanimous vote, to let no troops cross Sweden. Should such an attempt be made, not a single rail nor highway would be left intact. This final word left the Finns no choice.

On March 6, 1940, the Finnish delegation, headed by Prime Minister Ryti, flew to Stockholm and the following day arrived in Moscow. With him was the old veteran of the prewar negotiations, Juho Kusti Paasikivi, as well as General Rudolf Walden and Representative Väinö Voionmaa. German minister Blücher later wrote: "During that moment [when Finland was trying to decide whether or not to accept help] the fate of the entire world was in the hands of statesman Ryti. Large-scale political power groupings and the actual direction of history was based on Ryti's decisions."

President Kallio, in signing the credential authorizing the delegation to negotiate the cessation of hostilities, quoted from the Bible, "Woe to the idle shepherd that leaveth the flock! The sword shall be upon his arm, and upon his right eye: his arm shall be clean dried up, and his right eye shall be utterly darkened." (Zechariah 11:17)[1]

Stalin did not participate in any of the negotiations that otherwise had all the flavor of the prewar meetings; the cold dark rides to the Kremlin, frequently after midnight, heavy police security, and even heavier demands on the dignity and calm of the peace-seeking Finns. To meet with them were Molotov, Zhdanov, and General Vasiljev. The Finns considered it a bad sign that Zhdanov was there because he had been so adamant about moving borders away from Leningrad during the early propaganda days. But they consoled themselves with the fact that Kuusinen, at least, was absent.

Thus began a replay of the familiar territorial arguments with certain

---

[1]Five months later President Kallio's arm was paralyzed as the result of a stroke. In December, 1940, Kallio, now retired, collapsed at the Helsinki railroad station and died.

embellishmens added by Molotov. It would be a sleepless, round-the-clock exercise in futility by the Finn negotiators before a cease-fire could be agreed upon.

Meanwhile at the front there was no way of knowing when the dispute would be settled so the only thing to do was keep fighting.

16 | THE MIRACLE OF KOLLAA

At Kollaa no one thought much about peace. The loneliness and exhaustion was so awesome for each individual soldier strewn across the wilderness that he was aware of very little of the world's happenings. He only knew that Kollaa must hold. Against the Russians' great new offensive the numbed Finns became almost fanatical in their defense. They would fight to the last man. During these last days there were no fewer than twelve Russian divisions with 160,000 troops in the 100-square-mile area north of Ladoga. Opposing them were men like Captain Carl Von Haartman, battalion commander attached to the 34th Infantry Regiment; handsome, monocled, debonair soldier of fortune who had recently fought with Franco in Spain. With one leg shorter than the other because of an old wound, he was more of a gourmet than a skier. His command post became famous for the heavy aroma of spaghetti sauce and garlic. Under Von Haartman was hard-drinking, flamboyant Lieutenant Aarne Juutilainen, otherwise known as the "Terror of Morocco," because of his exploits with the French foreign legion.

And then there were men like Simo Häyhä, master shot of the 6th Company, who went out to "hunt Russians" each day. In civilian life Simo was a small farmer who had cabinets filled with trophies for marksmanship. In war he became the best known sniper in the Finnish army. Evenings he quietly cleaned his rifle and seldom said a word. He personally killed more than 500 Russians before he was seriously wounded.

Of this period Von Haartman said, "It is not difficult to lead a Finn battalion in battle. You know you have a handful of men under your command who can perform almost miraculous feats at times."

Some enlisted men had incredible nerves. Von Haartman describes the time he left his tent during a heavy Russian artillery barrage to investigate a mysterious sound that everyone had heard during the lulls between explosions. It was a rhythmic hissing noise and he wanted to satisfy his curiosity. "I had hardly made it through the tent area to the woods when I saw Private Kalle Pitkänen calmly sawing wood. I screamed, "What the hell are you doing sawing wood at a time like this? Don't you hear the Russian artillery firing all around us?"

Pitkänen looked up at me and pondered, "*Jahah*, if you say so." He put his saw against the wood pile, picked up his ax, and began chopping the wood. I didn't know whether to laugh or cry. Finally I said, "Why don't you put the ax away and come to my tent for coffee?"

Now as the Russian regiments advanced towards Tsuhmeikka and Kontro to attack the rear of the Kollaa defenders, other Russian tank divisions were pressuring the Finns at the Ulismainen swamps, trying to slash the road between Saarijärvi and Uomaa. The threat of being surrounded increased by the minute. Kollaa was weakening.

But the division commander, Antero Svensson, the stout, blond optimist, never lost his calm for a moment. He along with all the Kollaa defenders blindly believed that Kollaa would not fall. Even when the situation had seemed hopeless so many times in the past, the Finns had somehow managed to get some sort of help, so that by evening the lines were still intact. But by now the men were few; reinforcements were older troops who were unable to hold out the way the experienced defenders had. And under the murderous artillery fire from the Reds, these older men were swallowed up almost daily, sometimes even before they reached the line.

The Kollaa defenders continually pleaded with General Hägglund for more help. They needed at least a company, they said, for their planned counterattack. Hägglund finally sent word that the defenders of Ulismainen would be sent to Kollaa as soon as they had completed their mission. But when the Ulismainen battles were over, there were only a few men left in the company and these remnants did join the small forces who still believed in the miracle of Kollaa.

They waited for modern artillery and ammunition to arrive but what they received was two French 3.5-inch cannons, circa 1871. The shots could not be ignited by an electric fuse, even after the men tried three or four times. Finally they manually poked the gunpowder and shot into the barrel and fired it, only to have the shell explode perilously near their own troops. The aiming devices were so ancient that the men settled the problem simply by pointing the two relics toward the east.

Suddenly rumors of a cease-fire came from the front lines; now for the first time, the Kollaa defenders realized that foreign help was not coming after all. But whatever happened to the big Allied army? The world wants us to fight alone, they decided, and there would be applause for the brave Finns.

For the first time the Finnish counterassault did not succeed. The infantry was finished. The few men that were left never made it to the proper distance for throwing their hand grenades. They died of exhaustion and by Russian fire. The nerves of those who survived were gone.

Base Number 4 was given to the Russians. Even Killer Hill in the north was left behind where an entire Russian regiment of 4,000 attacked a Finnish platoon of 32 men. First Lieutenant Mäkipää with his messenger was forced to leave his artillery observation post, where he had directed the meager artillery fire since December, because dozens of Russians were crawling all over the hill. It was only through sheer luck and the effectiveness of several hand grenades that he and his messenger managed to escape from their position.

Oddly enough, the Finns who were still alive did not lose their faith. Vuorensola took his company from Ulismainen to Red House Hill, where he had fought before. The situation eased up somewhat, but after a horrible loss of Finn lives, a few of the men returned during the night. Everyone believed that the company commander and the rest of his soldiers were killed.

The following day another young company commander, a twenty-one-year-old lieutenant, returned with one man; all that was left of his company. Finally, two old experienced Kollaa fighters, Salo and Karkkainen, managed to find their way back. Word had gotten around that even the famed gymnast and Olympic representative, Make Uosikkinen, was dead.

The Finns could no longer fill the gaps in their lines because so many had been killed on their way to the breakthroughs.

In the command post the company commander looked at his map in the light of a hurricane lantern. The fire in the stove had gone out. He poked at the man lying next to the stove who he thought was asleep. But the man had died of his wounds. On the beds several wounded were lying

"The only way I can get a furlough is to get married or go to a funeral. I think I'll get married."
Cartoonist: JUSSI AARNIO. Published by Korven Kaiku. *Used by permission, Oy Lehmus, Tampere, Finland.*

side by side. In the opposite corner, on two of the bunk beds, dead bodies were piled up in layers. In the middle of the dugout some of the men were holding on to two soldiers who had lost their minds. They screamed and babbled incoherently as artillery shells hit the dugout's roof. The cries of the wounded, the last gasps of the dying now chimed in with the wild shouts of the hysterical soldiers.

The lights went out and the commanding officer began searching frantically for his lantern. He was the lone officer and it was his duty to draw up plans for a counterassault.

A platoon leader who had for the past two weeks led his troops successfully suddenly lost his nerve. He forced his way into the command dugout and stared at the officer with bloodshot eyes. "My wife is coming here with more machine guns. We're going to kill them all. Even the last one. My wife is coming with more machine guns." Then, he turned and ran into the open without his weapon or hat and screamed, "My wife is coming, my wife is coming, with more weapons!" A piece of red-hot shrapnel struck him, and he was quiet.

The Finnish command post, forty yards from the Russian dugout, was like a prison. The only way the company commander dared leave it was to first throw a few hand grenades toward the Russians to divert their attention.

Meanwhile, Colonel Pajari who had earlier led the Tolvajärvi-Aittojoki battles, visited with Colonel Svensson at Kollaa. Pajari promised two of his best battalions to be used for the destruction of the Russians at Tsuhmeikka. When that was accomplished, the battalions could remain at Kollaa.

They did come through the wilderness and scattered the Russians in all directions. But because they had no food supplies or a quartermaster corp with them, and being exhausted, they desperately needed a day of rest after the battles.

Meanwhile, the Kollaa defenders were given orders to withdraw several hundred feet. Salo and Karkkainen, who had been positioned near the railroad sector, discussed the situation with Lieutenants Leino and Laine. They had dug in on this evening of March 10 and the frontier was mysteriously quiet. Perhaps the Russians were tired; it was anybody's guess. New reservists arrived to swell their ranks. For the next two days the Finns busied themselves planning an over-all counterattack which would give the Russian division a final blow. Yes, they would attack.

But on the night of March 12 peace rumors that now seemed believable began circulating. The division commander's plan was never executed.

The lone Finnish soldier knew that he had to stay awake. His eyes must always be directed toward the Russians so that he could report immediately to the company. He was not sure who he would alert because he had not seen many of his own for days. He only knew that his people were there somewhere, because he hadn't seen anyone leaving. That's what the lieutenant had said when he was taken away on the stretcher.

They all die, he told himself. He would die also.

Only last night somebody had mentioned something about organizing a counteroffensive. Some new battalion would do the job. A whole new battalion had arrived and the Russians would be beaten once and for all. But where was the battlion? It was already midday. My God! Could they have died before they arrived?'

The soldier cried, and through his watery, stinging eyes, he watched the Russian side. He thought he saw the turrets of several tanks, but there were no people. Perhaps his eyes were lying, as they often did at night.

His legs felt weak, numb, and he could no longer stand upright in his trench. Now he could see dead Russians walking towards him. They were without guns and they were smiling. He suddenly felt himself slipping away into unconsciousness.

When he awoke, somebody was shaking him vigorously. A man he didn't know bent over him. The man had a narrow, bearded face and held a Russian automatic rifle in his hand. The Finn now realized that there was no artillery fire anymore. "Is this the death silence?" he asked.

"Get up soldier. We have peace," the man said.

"Will Kollaa hold?" the Finn asked. "It has to hold. Is the battalion coming? Is there going to be a counterassault?"

"It's peace now. Cease-fire. No more shooting. You can leave," the man said.

"Where are the others?"

"There are no others."

Finally the soldier understood that nobody was shooting anymore. But he couldn't believe that peace had really come. He lapsed into unconsciousness again.

When he came to, he felt somebody putting sugar into his mouth, and now there were people he could recognize. Some of the men were lying on the roadside and some were standing on their skis.

Peace must be true. There was no shooting.

But all of the men looked so unhappy. Had there been some kind of accident?

Somebody mentioned the unbelievably hard peace terms and it was clear to the soldier that this was why everyone looked so sad.

"But why this?" he asked. "We did not give in at Kollaa. Kollaa did hold."[1]

[1]Based on material from *Kollaa Kestää'* by Erkki Palolampi (Helsinki: Werner Söderström, 1940).

17 | FINLAND IN MOURNING

Flags flew at half mast in Helsinki and all other Finnish cities. People walked the streets with tearful eyes; some even said that the most welcome sound they could hear would be an air-raid siren. On March 13, 1940, Finland was the saddest country in the world. She mourned her 25,000 dead and 55,000 wounded; she grieved for the material losses even in the face of moral victories that her gallant men had fought so hard to achieve. Finland was now at the mercy of Russia, and she listened again to what men of mightier nations had to say. There were, for instance, the ringing words of Winston Churchill:

Finland alone—in danger of death, superb, sublime Finland—shows what free men can do. The service that Finland has rendered to humanity is magnificent .... We cannot say what Finland's fate will be, but nothing could be sadder to the rest of the civilized world than that this splendid northern race should at the end be destroyed and, in the face of incredible odds, should fall into a slavery worse than death.

Foreign Minister Väinö Tanner said, "Peace has been restored, but what kind of peace? Henceforth our country will continue to live as a mutilated nation."

As the men skied home from the battlefields, many of them wept at the appalling peace terms. They were tired from the strain, but they still considered themselves an unbeaten army. Many wondered how they would feel when they had been given time to rest and reflect.

When the peace delegation returned to Helsinki on March 14, they found their city in a bewildered apathy. Peace, under such terms, was unreal . . . horrible.

In Russia, one general is said to have commented, "We have won enough ground to bury our dead . . ."

The Russians had had plenty of time to make their plans, to choose the time and place for attack, and they far outnumbered their neighbor. Yet as Khrushchev wrote: ". . . even in these most favorable conditions it was only after great difficulty and enormous losses that we were finally able to win. A victory at such a cost was actually a moral defeat."

Out of the total of 1.5 million men sent to Finland, one million of them (according to Khrushchev) were killed. They lost close to 1,000 aircraft, 2,300 tanks and armored cars, and an enormous amount of other war materials including munitions, automobiles, trucks, and horses.[1]

Finnish casualties, though proportionately light, were a staggering loss to a nation of 4 million people. A similar situation in the United States in 1940 with its population of over 130 million people would have seen 2.6 *million* Americans dead or wounded in just 105 days.

As the terms of the peace treaty were being settled, Molotov remarked: "Since blood has been shed against the Soviet government's wishes and without Russia's being to blame, the territorial concessions Finland offered must be greater than those proposed by Russia in Moscow in October and November of 1939."

Under the peace treaty, Russia took Finland's second biggest city, Viipuri; her largest Arctic Ocean port, Petsamo; the strategic area of Hanko; her largest lake, Ladoga; and the entire Karelian Isthmus, the home of 12 percent of Finland's population.

Finland relinquished a total of 22,000 square miles of land to the Russians. In addition to Viipuri she lost such vital ports as Uuras, Koivisto, the northern part of Lake Ladoga, and the important Saimaa canal. Two weeks were allowed for the evacuation of the population and its property; much was left behind or destroyed. The greatest economic loss in Karelia was the timber industry with its fine sawmills and veneer and wood refining plants. Also, Finland lost much of her chemical, textile, and metal industries, 10 percent of which was in the Vuoksi Valley. Nearly one hundred power stations were turned over to the victorious Soviets.

---

[1]Estimates of Russian material losses varied. The authors have chosen to use those of Marshal Mannerheim. Carl Gustav Mannerheim, *The Memoirs of Marshal Mannerheim* (London: Cassell & Co. Ltd., 1953), pp. 369–370.

In his radio speech to the people of Finland, President Kallio reminded everyone of the great responsibilities which remained to be borne by the dependents of the fallen; the war invalids and other victims and for the population of areas which were now a part of Russia. The people in the ceded areas would be given the right to determine for themselves whether to leave their homes or stay and become a part of the Soviet Union.

Not a single Finn accepted the latter, even though 450,000 of them were left destitute and homeless by the peace treaty. The Finnish government requisitioned every possible vehicle to evacuate the refugees, and temporary homes were arranged for them in other parts of Finland. Many of these people were in need of public assistance because more than half of them had made their livings from agriculture: 40,000 farms would have to be found, and it was Finland's collective responsibility to see that this was done. On June 28, 1940, the Emergency Resettlement Act was passed which provided for the refugees.

The question of why Russia signed the peace treaty with no real intention of occupying Finland was debated for years after the war. Khrushchev says that Stalin showed statesmanly wisdom here because he knew that "Finland wasn't relevant to the basic needs of the world proletarian revolution."

But the tremendous defense effort of the Finns undoubtedly had much to do with Stalin's decisions to bow out when he did. Subjugating the people of this stubborn, hostile nation would be an awkward task where guerrilla activities were certain to continue indefinitely.

On a larger scale, Stalin dared not allow territorially narrow Finland to grow into a world war, for he had no intention of going to war against the Allies on the German side. With the Finnish frontier still unbroken, with technical help and war materials from the Allies, the Finns could easily have held out until spring at which time a Soviet breakthrough might have been more costly than ever.

The Winter War had considerable impact on the fluctuating plans of the great powers. For Britain's Prime Minister Neville Chamberlain, the vacillation of his government during this period of "mid-winter madness" led to his downfall seven weeks later at the time of the Nazi invasion of Norway and Denmark. The French government of Daladier fell one week after the Norway-Denmark take-over with Pierre Laval using the Finnish conflict as his wedge to gain power.

For the Germans, had the Soviet Union not appeared so unfavorable,

Hitler would hardly have underestimated the war potential of the Russians to the extent he did. Considering the enormous effort put forth by the Soviets in Finland, very little was received in the way of results.

In spite of the fact that half of the regular Russian divisions in Europe and western Siberia were mobilized against their small neighbor, the Red Army failed badly, and for very obvious reasons.

According to Marshal Mannerheim: "It was a characteristic mistake of the Red high command to start military operations without paying necessary attention to the basic factors in the war against Finland; the character of the theater of war and the strength of the enemy."[2] The latter was weak in material, but the Russians did not realize that their army organization was too cumbersome for fighting in the northern wilderness in deep winter. Mannerheim points out that they could have experimented in conditions similar to those they would encounter in Finland, but they did not because of their blind faith in modern technology. Emulating the Germans on the plains of Poland would not work in a land of forests.

Another mistake was the use of political commissars within the combatant ranks. "That every order must first be approved by the political leaders necessarily led to delay and confusion, not to speak of lessening of initiative and fear of responsibility," Mannerheim later wrote. "The fact that surrounded units refused to surrender in spite of cold and hunger was largely due to the political commissars. Soldiers were prevented from surrendering by threats of reprisals against their families and the assurance that they would be killed or tortured if they fell into the hands of the enemy. There were innumerable cases where officers as well as men preferred suicide to surrender."[3]

Although the Russian officers were brave men, there was a kind of inertia in the higher ranks which excluded maneuvering in the stubborn pursuit of victory or defeat. "There was a striking absence of creative imagination where the fluctuations of the situation demanded quick decisions . . . " Although the Russian infantryman showed himself brave, tough, and frugal, he too lacked initiative. "Contrary to his Finnish adversary, he was a mass fighter who was incapable of independent action when out of contact with his officers or comrades."[4] Mannerheim attrib-

[2]Carl Gustav Mannerheim, *The Memoirs of Marshal Mannerheim* (London: Cassell & Co. Ltd., 1953), p. 366.
[3]Ibid., p. 367.
[4]Ibid.

utes this to the Russian people's hard struggle against nature which in the course of ages had created a capacity for suffering and deprivation, a passive courage, and a fatalism incomprehensible to Europeans.

There was no doubt that the experiences of the Finnish campaign were made full use of by Marshal Timoshenko in his reorganization of the Red Army. In his own words, "the Russians have learned much in this hard war in which the Finns fought with heroism."

From the Soviet point of view, Marshall S. S. Biriuzov wrote:

The storming of the Mannerheim Line was regarded as a model of operational and tactical art. Troops were taught to overcome the enemy's protracted defense by a gradual accumulation of forces and a patient "gnawing through" of breaches in the enemy's fortifications in accordance with all the rules of engineering science. Insufficient attention was paid to questions of co-operation among different branches and services of the armed forces under rapidly changing conditions. We had to retrain ourselves under enemy fire, paying a high price for the experience and knowledge without which we could not beat Hitler's army.[5]

Admiral N. G. Kuznetsov summed up, "We had received a severe lesson. We had to profit by it. The Finnish campaign had shown that organization of military leadership at the center left much to be desired. In case of war (large or small) one had to know in advance who would be the supreme commander in chief, and what apparatus he would work through; was it to be a specially created organ or the general staff as it had operated in peacetime? These were by no means secondary questions."[6]

As to the far-reaching effects of the Winter War on the performance of the Red Army against Hitler, Chief Marshal of Artillery N. N. Voronov stated:

At the end of March [1940] a plenary session of the central committee of the party was held, at which a good deal of attention was devoted to examining the lessons of the war. It noted serious shortcomings in the operations of our forces and in the indoctrination and training of our troops. We had still not learned how to make use of the full potential of the new equipment. The slipshod work of the rear services was criticized. The troops were ill-prepared for operations in forests and for coping with freezing weather and impassable roads. The Party demanded that the combat experience accumulated in Khasan, at Khalkhin Gol [Khalka River], and on the Karelian Isthmus be thoroughly taken into account,

[5]S.S.Biriuzov, *Kogda gremeli pushki* (Moscow, 1961), pp. 31–32.
[6]N.G.Kuznetsov, *"Pered voinoi"* (Oktiabr, 1965), pp. 188–89.

that armaments be perfected and that the training of the troops be improved. It became necessary to revise the regulations and manuals in a short time and to make them correspond to the demands of modern warfare. . . . Artillery material was of particular concern. During the freezing weather in Finland, the semi-automatic mechanisms in the guns failed. New types of lubricants had to be developed immediately. When the temperatures dropped sharply, the 15-mm. howitzer behaved in an erratic manner. Large-scale research work had to be carried out.[7]

Khrushchev said: "All of us—and Stalin first and foremost—sensed in our victory a defeat by the Finns. It was a dangerous defeat because it encouraged our enemies' conviction that the Soviet Union was a colossus with feet of clay. . . . We had to draw some lessons for the immediate future from what had happened."[8]

Following the Winter War, political commissars were officially abolished and the rank of general and other ranks were reintroduced into the Red Army, with the privileges attached to them.

For the Finns the Winter War had been epic and glorious in spite of the final disaster. For the next fifteen months they went through a state of half-peace, until finally, undisguised hatred of the Soviet Union got the better of reason and judgment. This was matched by an almost pathological Russian suspicion of Finland. During this period a heavy cloak of secrecy surrounded all government activities outside of Finland; censorship prevented the populace from knowing exactly what was going on beyond their borders. They were convinced that Hitler was in the final stages of defeating Britain, while the old Soviet menace was still at their doorstep.

Because of their earlier gratitude to Germany for helping them in their struggle for independence and because Germany offered them badly needed supplies, the Finns sided with Germany in the hope of recovering their lost territories. After several warnings, Britain declared war on Finland in December 1941, but the two forces never met in combat. There was no formal alliance with Germany; the Finnish and German armies fought under separate commands and there was little or no co-operation between the two military forces.

[7]N. N. Voronov, *Na sluzhbe voennoi* (Moscow, 1963), pp. 153–57.

[8]*Khrushchev Remembers* (Boston: Little Brown and Company, 1970), pp. 157–58.

Many Finnish soldiers lost their initial enthusiasm in this so-called Continuation War, once their old borders were regained. In September, 1944, the war with the USSR came to an end. The Finns rid themselves of the Germans on their soil but lost Karelia forever, along with various other areas.

Reparations to Russia for both the Winter War and the Continuation War were enormous, but the Finns paid them. Their stoic reasoning was, "The East took our men, the Germans took our women, the Swedes took our children. But at least we are left with our war debt."

Finland's stand against the Soviet Union during the Winter War must remain among the most stirring in history.

EPILOGUE: SNOW COVERS
THE TRACKS

Many winter snows have fallen on the bloody battlefields of the Winter War. The sadness and grief brought on by this war have now given way to more practical considerations. The true front line soldier does not hate or despise an enemy who bravely and honestly fights him to the end. In this sense the Finnish soldier will give his Russian adversaries his sincere respect. Their bravery and endurance against cold, hunger, and hopelessness and their acceptance of the Russian military discipline were admirable, sometimes even awesome. On the other hand, perhaps the Russians, now that they have had their big battle for their Fatherland, understand what the Winter War meant to the Finns, and see that Viipuri, Salmi and Raate Road were our "Volokolamski highways," and Summa, Kitelä, Tolvajärvi, and Suomussalmi were Finland's small Stalingrads.

From the humane point of view, the end result of this war perhaps should have compensated us better for our efforts and sacrifices. But being a straightforward people and being used to the thought that it is more important to fight well than to win, the loser is proud of his brave battle. If war and peace could be decided by the front line soldier, wars would be few and far between, and peace would be just. He knows the horrors of war and gives credit to his adversaries' efforts and accomplishments.

With these thoughts, the Finnish soldier of the Winter War can now say to his former adversary: "Step into my house. Let us reminisce about the past. There is something here that I can put on the table for us to share. I have hung my knife on the wall, so would you leave your ax on the porch?"

—Colonel Y. A. Järvinen, Finnish army

(Free translation, used by permission.)

"I still say we won, dammit!"
Cartoonist: Jussi Aarnio. *Used by permission, Oy Lehmus, Tampere, Finland.*

APPENDIX A: ASSISTANCE FROM WINTER WAR PARTICIPANTS

Several Finnish newspapers succeeded in putting the authors in touch with Winter War participants; *Aamulehti* and *Kansanlehti* in Tampere and *Uusi Suomi* in Helsinki. Through this media, the authors were able to share the experiences of those who were on the scene. Few have been identified by name in the book, yet they will surely recognize their personal stories. The participants' names are listed, along with their present locations and where and in what capacity they served in the Winter War.

TOIVO ALIO, Koivistonkylä; Kollaanjoki, Hyrsylä; Infantry
G. ANERO, Kulju; Summa, Karelian Isthmus; Artillery Communications
HEIKKI EEROLA, Ritvala; Suomussalmi; Infantry Squad Leader
TOIVO HEIKKILÄ, Tampere; Taipale, Karelian Isthmus; Infantry
VÄINÖ HEISKA, Kunnas; Northern Finland; Quartermaster Corps
MARTTI HUHTA, Eräjärvi; Karelian Isthmus; Medic
LAURI HUHTAJÄRVI, Korkeakoski; Summa, Karelian Isthmus; Rifleman
VEIKKO Jalonen, Helsinki; Summa, Karelian Isthmus; Rifleman
JALMARI KIINTONEN, Tampere; Suomussalmi, Kuhmo; Rifleman
VÄINÖ KOSTIAINEN, Kulju; Summa, Karelian Isthmus; Anti-Panzer
ERKKI KOUKKU, Savonlinna; Karelian Isthmus; Artillery Communications
KUSTAA KULJUNEN, Tampere; Summa, Viipuri; Rifleman
PEKKA KUUSINIEMI, Kolho; Tolvajärvi; Rifleman
VESTERI LEPISTÖ, Kihniö; Rifleman
MATTI LINNA, Viiala; Sergeant Major, Finnish air force
JORMA NAPOLA, Haukilahti; Summa, Karelian Isthmus; Anti-Panzer
HEIKKI OSARA, Vesajärvi, Summa, Karelian Isthmus; Rifleman

SULO RAJALA, Tampere; Viipuri, Karelian Isthmus; Patrol Leader
LAURI RANTA, Sahalahi; Karelian Isthmus; Rifleman
TOIVO ROSSI, Tampere; Suomussalmi; Mortar Man
LAURA VEVARI, Karvia; East Karelian Isthmus; Cook
VILHO VIRTA, Tampere; Summa; Sommee; Viipuri; Machine gunner

APPENDIX B: HELP
FROM ABROAD

Ammunition, weapons, etc., actually purchased by Finland, as reported by Juho Niukkanen, Finland's Defense Minister during the Winter War.

FROM SWEDEN:

Received in January 1940	8	75-mm. field cannon
Received in February 1940	48	75-mm. field cannon and 27,000 rounds
Received during the war	17	105-mm. field cannon and 5200 rounds
	12	150-mm. howitzers and 4000 rounds
	4	210-mm. howitzers and 400 rounds
	9	175-mm. anti-aircraft cannon
	76	40-mm. anti-aircraft cannon and 144,000 rounds
	18	37-mm. anti-panzer cannon, 45,000 rounds
	100	machine guns
	77,000	rifles and 17,000,000 bullets
	8	training aircraft
	8	bomber aircraft (old models)
	12	Gladiator aircraft (all to Swedish volunteers).
	8,000	volunteers

FROM FRANCE:

Received during the war	12	155-mm. howitzers and 12,000 rounds
	12	105-mm. field cannon and 54,000 rounds
	100	81-mm. mortars and 200,000 rounds
	40	25-mm. anti-panzer cannon and 25,000 rounds
	150	radios
	5,000	automatic rifles and 11,000,000 bullets
	20,000	hand grenades
	12	tractors
	136	old vintage cannon and 300,500 rounds
	76	Moran and Kolhoven fighter aircraft
(Only 12 received)	36	75-mm. field cannon and 50,000 rounds
(Not received)	10	47-mm. anti-panzer cannon and 5,000 rounds

FROM UNION OF SOUTH AFRICA:

| Received during the war | 25 | Gloster Gladiator aircraft (gift) |

FROM ENGLAND:

Received during the war	20	torpedos
	450	mines
	12	152-mm. mobile naval guns
	25	114-mm. howitzers and 25,000 rounds
	24	76-mm. anti-aircraft cannon, and 72,000 rounds
	18	40-mm. anti-aircraft cannon and 36,000 rounds
	24	13-mm. anti-aircraft cannon and 72,000 rounds
	200	14-mm. anti-panzer rifles
	28	tractors
	20,000,000	rifle bullets
	10,000,000	pistol bullets

	40,000	hand grenades
	50,000	"sympathy" uniforms[1]
		bombs, field kitchens, tents, communication equipment, etc.
	33	Gloster Gladiator aircraft
	12	Hurricane aircraft
	17	Lysander reconnaissance aircraft
	24	Blenheim bomber aircraft
	230	volunteers
(Not received)	4	torpedo boats
	30	84-mm. field cannon

FROM USA:[2]

(Only a few received during the war)	44	Brewster aircraft
(Arrived in Norway after the war)	32	203-mm. howitzers
	200	75-mm. field cannon
(Arrived two days before the war ended)	350	volunteers

FROM DENMARK:

Received during the war	178	20-mm. Madsen anti-aircraft cannon (bullets were ordered from England)
	2	volunteer fighter pilots (both were killed)
		rucksacks, preserves etc.
	800	volunteers

FROM NORWAY:

Received during the war	50,000	pairs of shoes
	100,000	rucksacks (50,000 as a gift)
	16,000	blankets

[1]The 50,000 "sympathy" uniforms from the British could not be used in combat because of their similarity to the brown uniforms of the Russians. They were, however, greatly appreciated by the home front.

[2]Negotiations for additional material were canceled after March 13, 1940.

200,000	kilos of sheetmetal, cannon harness, saddles, etc
800	volunteers
12	75-mm. field cannon and 7,166 rounds

FROM HUNGARY:

Received during the war	40	40-mm. anti-aircraft cannon and 10,000 rounds
	30	8-mm. anti-panzer rifles
	300,000	hand grenades
	32,500	rounds for 81-mm. mortars
	20,000	rounds for 20-mm. anti-aircraft cannon
	6,000	rounds for 37-mm. anti-panzer cannon
	450	volunteers

FROM GERMANY:

Received just before the war	30	20-mm. anti-aircraft cannon and 100,000 rounds

---

FROM ITALY:

Received during the war	35	45-cm. torpedos
	150	mines
	20	tractors
	100	81-mm. mortars and 75,000 rounds
	12	76-mm. anti-aircraft cannon and 24,000 rounds
	48	20-mm. anti-aircraft cannon and 384,000 rounds
	12	47-mm. anti-panzer cannon and 25,000 rounds
	6,000	pistols
(Only 28 received, 148 remained in Norway)	176	flamethrowers
(Only 17 received, February 27, 1940)	35	Fiat aircraft
Arrived during the war	150	volunteers, including one fighter pilot who was killed

(Not received)   5   torpedo boats
                            100,000   rifles and 50,000,000 bullets

---

FROM BELGIUM:

Received during the war   700   automatic rifles and 10,000 bullets
                              2,456   9-mm. pistols and 11,000,000 bullets
                              5,000   7.65-mm. pistols and 1,080,000 bullets

---

 # APPENDIX C: COMPARATIVE STRENGTH AND STRUCTURE OF THE FINNISH AND RUSSIAN DIVISION

The Finnish division consisted of headquarters, staff, three infantry regiments, one light brigade, one field artillery regiment, two engineering companies, one communication company, one line fortification company, one quartermaster company. Total manpower, approximately 14,200 men.

The Russian division consisted of three infantry regiments, one field artillery regiment, one howitzer regiment, one anti-panzer battery, one reconnaissance battalion, one communications battalion, one engineering battalion. Total manpower, approximately 17,500 men.

Weaponry for a Finnish and a Russian division:

	FINNISH	RUSSIAN
Rifles	11,000	14,000
Submachine guns	250	none
Automatic rifles	250	419
Machine guns (7.62-mm.)	116	200
Anti-aircraft machine guns, 4 barrels	none	32
Machine guns (12.7-mm.)	none	6
Rifle mortars	none	261
Mortars (81- to 82-mm.)	18	18
Mortars (120-mm.)	none	12
Field artillery (37- to 45-mm.)	18	48
Field artillery (75- to 90-mm.)	24	38

	FINNISH	RUSSIAN
Field artillery (105- to 152-mm.)	12	40
Tanks	none	40–50
Armored cars	none	15

In a division, as far as machine guns and mortars were concerned, Russia had twice the firepower of the Finns and their artillery was three times as strong. The Red Army had no submachine guns but that was balanced partially by their automatic and semi-automatic rifles. Support artillery was available to Russian divisions at the request of the high command; there were numerous panzer brigades available and a seemingly unlimited supply of ammunition.

APPENDIX D: LOCATION OF RUSSIAN AND FINNISH DIVISIONS

90-mile front from Finnish Gulf to Lake Ladoga at Karelian Isthmus

RUSSIAN		FINNISH
53d	136th	4th
86th	62d	3d
43d	97th	5th
70th	17th	23d
113th	8th	1st
7th	4th	2d
138th	50th	21st
24th	142d	8th
100th	150th	7th
59th	49th	
123d		
40th		
84th		
51st		
90th		
80th		

600-mile front from Lake Ladoga to Arctic Ocean

RUSSIAN	AREA	FINNISH
168th		
72d	Salmi	
25th	Uomaa	
11th	Syskylake	13th
37th	Kitelä	
18th	Lemetti	
60th		
56th	Kollaa	
128th	Tolvajärvi	
164th	Suojärvi	12th
75th	Ägläjärvi	
139th		
		25th Inf. Reg.
155th	Lieksa, Ilomantsi	2 reinforced
54th	Kuhmo	Battalions (12th and 13th)
163d	Suomussalmi	9th Div.
44th	Raate Road	minus 1 Reg.
122d	Salla	40th Inf. Reg.
88th		
104th	Petsamo	1 reinforced
52d		Battalion

(Many special Russian Panzer and Artillery Regiments, in addition to the regular Division and Regimental Panzer and Artillery units, not included)

 # APPENDIX E: UNDERSTANDING PLACE NAMES IN FINLAND

The following is a list of suffixes with phonetic pronunciation. The accent is on the first syllable in each case:

saari: island (sah-ri)
järvi: lake (yar-vi)
salmi: strait or narrow (sahl-mi)
niemi: peninsula (ni-ay-me)
suu: mouth, as of a river (soo)
koski: waterfall ("o" as in oval)
vaara: mountain ridge (var-ah)
kylä: village (ky-lah)
lahti: bay or inlet (lah-te)
vesi: small bodies of water (vay-see)
selkä: any wide stretch of water (sel-kah)
ylä: meaning upper (eye-lah)
ala: meaning lower (ah-la)
pohjola: north (poh-yoy-la)
etelä: south (ay-tel-ah)

These suffixes, added as integral parts of place names, have special meanings as keys to terrain and geographical features. For instance, joki (pronounced yoki) which means river: Taipaleenjoki or Taipale River. The middle syllable, "en," denotes the genitive form.

162

BIBLIOGRAPHY

BOOKS

AARNIO, MATTI A. *Talvi Sodan Ihme* [The Miracle of the Winter War]. Jyväskylä, Finland: K. J. Gummerus, 1966.

BIALER, SEWERYN, ed. *Stalin and His Generals.* New York: Pegasus, 1969.

CITRINE, WALTER MCLENNAN. *My Finnish Diary.* New York: Penguin Books, 1940.

CLARK, DOUGLAS. *Liittoutuneet Lähtevät Talvisotaan* [The Allies Go to the Winter War]. Helsinki: Otava, 1966.

ERHO, KAARLO. *Summa.* Porvoo, Finland: Werner Söderström, 1940.

FIRSOFF, WOLDEMAR AXEL. *Ski Track on the Battlefield.* New York: A. S. Barnes, 1943.

HAARLA, LAURI. *Idän Laumoja Päin;* Yksinäytöksinen Näytelmä Suomalais-venäläisestä Sodasta [Against the Eastern Hordes]. Helsinki: Otava, 1940.

HAARTMAN, CARL VON. *Francon Armeijasta Kollaanjoelle* [From Franco's Army to the Kollaa River]. Helsinki: Otava, 1940.

HALL, WENDY. *The Finns and Their Country.* London: Max Parrish, 1967.

HALSTI, WOLF. *Talvisota, 1939-40* [The Winter War, 1939-40]. Helsinki: Otava, 1957.

HANNULA, JOOSE OLAVI. *Neuvostoliitto Hyökkää Pohjolaan: Suomenvenäjän Talvisota* [The Soviet Union Attacks the North]. Helsinki: Suomen Kirja, 1944.

HINSHAW, DAVID. *Heroic Finland.* New York: G. P. Putnam's Sons, 1952.

JAKOBSON, MAX. *The Diplomacy of the Winter War.* Cambridge, Mass.: Harvard Univ. Press 1961.

KAARELA, ELSA, ed. *Tuntematon Suomalainen Sotilas* [Unkown Finnish Soldier]. Helsinki: Otava, 1941.

JÄRVINEN, Y. A. *Suomalainen ja Venäläinen Taktiikka Talvisodassa* [Finnish and Russian Tactics in the Winter War]. Porvoo and Helsinki: Werner Söderström, 1948.

KARUNKI, PEKKA. *Vaipuneet Kotkat* [Fallen Eagles]. Porvoo, Finland: Werner Söderström, 1940.

KARHUNEN, JOPPE. *Kotkia Kuolin Syoksyissa* [Eagle's Dive to Death]. Helsinki: Otava, 1968.

KORHONEN, ARVI, ed. *Viisi Sodan Vuotta* [Five Years of War]. Porvoo, Finland: Werner Söderström, 1963.

KHRUSHCHEV, NIKITA. *Khrushchev Remembers.* Boston: Little, Brown and Co., 1970.

LEHMUS, ESKO. *Nauru Sodalle* [Laugh at the War]. Tampere, Finland: Kustannus Lehmus, 1961.

LUUKKANEN, EINO. *Fighter Over Finland.* London: Macdonald and Co., 1963.

MANNERHEIM, CARL GUSTAV. *The Memoirs of Marshal Mannerheim.* London: Cassell and Co., Ltd., 1953.

MAZOUR, ANATOLE G. *Finland Between East and West.* Princeton, New Jersey: D. Van Nostrand, 1956.

MIIHKALI, ONTTONI. *Suomussalmen Sotatanterilla.* [At the Battlefields of Suomussalmi]. Hämeenlinna, Finland: Karisto, 1940.

MINISTRY OF FOREIGN AFFAIRS OF FINLAND. *The Finnish Bluebook.* Philadelphia and New York: J.B. Lippincott Co., 1940.

MORNE, HAKAN. *Ärans Winter* [Winter of Honor]. Berlin: Universitas Verlag, P. Schmid, 1942.

NIUKKANEN, JUHO. *Talvisodan Puolustus-Ministeri Kertoo* [The Defense Minister's Account of the Winter War]. Porvoo, Finland: Werner Söderström, 1951.

O'BALLANCE, EDGAR. *The Red Army.* New York: Frederick Praeger, 1964.

OTT, ESTRID. *Med Lotterne bag Fronten.* [With the Lottas Behind the Front]. København: S. Hasselbalch, 1940.

PALOLAMPI, ERKKI. *Kollaa Kestää* [Kollaa Will Hold]. Helsinki: Werner Söderström, 1940.

RINTALA, MARVIN. *Four Finns.* Berkeley and Los Angeles: University of California Press, 1969.

SALMI, VILJO. *Tulilinjojen Ihme* [Miracle of the Front Lines]. Porvoo, Finland: Werner Söderström, 1940.

SIILASVUO, H. J. *Suomussalmen Taistelut* [The Battles of Suomussalmi]. Helsinki: Otava, 1940.

TANNER, VAINO. *Olin Ulkoministerinä Talvisodan Aikana* [I Was the Foreign Minister During the Winter War]. Helsinki: Tammi, 1951.

WARD, EDWARD, 7th Viscount Bangor. *Despatches from Finland: January-April, 1940.* London: John Lane, 1940.

WARNER, OLIVER. *Marshal Mannerheim and the Finns*. London: Weidenfeld and Nicolson, 1967.

ZENZINOV, VLADIMIR MIKHAILOVICH. *Vstrecha s Rossiei: kak i chem zhivut v Sovetskom Sojiuzie; pis 'ma v krasniu armiiu 1939-40* [227 Letters Found on Dead Russian Soldiers on the Battlefields of Finland]. New York: privately printed, 1944.

PERIODICALS

The New York Times, November 15, 1939, through April, 1940.
Izvestia, November 15, 1939, through April, 1940.
Pravda, November 15, 1939, through April, 1940.

INDEX